Dig This!

Landscaping
Without a Backhoe
or a Big Budget
for Northern
California
and Beyond

Kate Anchordoguy

SASQUATCH BOOKS
SEATTLE

For my mother, who has always believed in me.
—K. A.

Printed in the United States of America
Published by Sasquatch Books
Distributed by Publishers Group West
08 07 06 05 04 03   6 5 4 3 2 1

Cover design: Kate Basart
Interior design: Stewart A. Williams
Interior illustrations: Bill Evans
Copy editor: Alice Copp Smith

Library of Congress Cataloging in Publication Data
Anchordoguy, Kate.
        Dig this! : landscaping without a backhoe or a big budget / Kate Anchordoguy.
            p. cm.
        Includes bibliographical references.
        ISBN 1-57061-338-9
        1. Landscape gardening. I. Title
        SB473 .A518 2003
        712—dc21   2002191117

Sasquatch Books
119 South Main Street, Suite 400
Seattle, Washington 98104
(206) 467-4300
www.sasquatchbooks.com
books@sasquatchbooks.com

Contents

Introduction

I have landscaped hundreds of yards—many of them probably a lot like yours. It's a little embarrassing to think back to some of my earliest attempts at this trade. On our first paying job, my business partner Jeanne and I hand-pulled every weed in a neighbor's front yard, hour after endless hour, till there was only dirt. We ended up making all of thirty-nine cents an hour each. Of course, this was back in 1978, but even then it was plain we weren't going to get rich very quickly.

Later that summer, we landed our first real installation, a small back yard in Benicia. I was so thrilled that the clients wanted *us* to put in their yard—I was only twenty, after all, with just enough knowledge to make me dangerous. As it turned out, I hadn't noticed that the yard was accessible only by several flights of steps. Up. In fact, it wasn't until the topsoil was delivered that the gravity of our situation really sank in. How were we going to get all that dirt from the driveway into the back yard? By garbage can, as it turned out. Half-full garbage cans, Jeanne on one side and me on the other, laboring up and up and up those stairs, resting for panting breaks on every landing, over and over for *days*, or so it seemed.

Oh, the mistakes I've made, the traumas I've suffered, the humiliations, indignities, and exhaustion I've endured. I've broken waterlines with picks. I've broken them with trenchers. I've smashed more fingers than I can count, and dropped boulders on my feet. I've bashed in radiators and set fire to a street. I even ran over three pieces of brand new equipment *in one go*.

I've blown up drip lines, sliced through timer wires, and screwed valves in backwards. I've fried hydrangeas and drowned manzanitas. In the summer, I've choked on dust, pulled stickers from my socks, and passed out from heat exhaustion. In the winter, I've sprained my forearms shoveling mud the consistency of library paste.

Worst of all, I've needlessly expended millions of calories. A lot of my toil—especially in the early, learning years—was simply wasted effort. I squandered immeasurable time and energy before figuring out easier and more efficient ways to work. I've invented and then *reinvented* the wheel. I've even experimented with dogsleds, the travois, snowshoes, pogo sticks . . .

If wisdom is measured by the mistakes we've made, I am very, very wise.

Let the cost of this book be the only price *you* pay for wisdom. I want to minimize *your* expenditures of time, money, and labor as I help you create a garden that works well and looks great. I also want you to have as much fun landscaping as I do. I will try to anticipate your every mistake, and warn you with flashing lights and honking horns of the dangers that lie ahead. Here's the route we'll take.

In Chapter 1, I'll show you how to plan well, shop intelligently, and work efficiently. In the second chapter, I'll help you design a landscape that fulfills your needs and dreams without busting your budget. In Chapter 3, I'll give a brief overview of some of the more common types of construction projects, with special emphasis on their timing in relation to the installation of the landscape as a whole. Chapter 4 is devoted to the oft-ignored but essential task of shaping the earth itself by focusing on the movement of water throughout your yard. In Chapter 5, you'll learn how to make your soil hospitable to plant life. In the sixth chapter, I'll take you carefully and gently through the complexities of designing and installing your very own (functioning) irrigation system. In Chapter 7, you'll learn how to plant like a pro. Chapter 8, in which I guide you through the installation and renovation of lawns, finishes the book.

I should warn you that most of my twenty-five-plus years of landscaping experience (I don't count the gardens I made as a child in Libya and New Mexico) have been in one region—California's Bay Area. In particular, I'm very familiar with soil and climatic conditions in Contra Costa, Solano, Marin, and

Sonoma Counties. So if you'll be landscaping elsewhere—in San Mateo, Eureka, or even Minnesota—you'll want to take into account the specific regional characteristics of your own particular piece of the planet. I think most of the tenets of this book will hold true for a broader geographical scope than that of the Bay Area, but as you read you'll want to factor in local site conditions—the amount and timing of rainfall, and extremes of hot and cold temperatures, for example. If I suggest soaking the ground before working it, and it's rained every day for the last two weeks, just ignore that part, okay?

Seat belts fastened? We'll start out slow, emphasizing overall processes and strategies rather than specific techniques.

Chapter 1

Planning Your Project

The Four Rules of Engagement

To many people, "planning" means designing—that is, determining the actual form of the garden: where the lawn goes, how wide the paths are, and so on. We'll do this in Chapter 2, Basic Landscape Design. At this stage in the game, we are more interested in a different sort of planning: organizing the project as a whole, breaking it down into phases, and establishing timelines.

RULE NO. 1: PLAN WELL

Your landscape project will likely follow the order of the chapters in this book. After planning the project, the next step is always to design the garden. Then, generally, you grade, install irrigation, prepare the soil, and plant. If yours is an older home, there may be lots of stuff to tear out before you officially break ground. And you will probably have a few construction projects sandwiched in between these stages (the timing of which is the primary focus of Chapter 3, Phasing the Construction).

Depending on the budgets for all three of your resources—time, money, and energy—you may decide to landscape your yard in two or more distinct phases. Perhaps in the first year you will draw up a design, grade, and get your major trees planted. Then the following season you may install your irrigation, complete the planting, and mulch. There are many ways—and no one correct way—to break the job down into manageable bites.

As Time Goes "Bye"

Project planning is primarily a way of managing your first resource, time. For example, if you know that you want to break ground in the spring, you should probably begin working on your design the winter before. Or you can work your way backwards from a specific date in the future by which the garden must be completed—perhaps a special birthday party, or a wedding.

How do you know how much time it will take to do your yard? Even I, who have been landscaping for more years than I care to count, and whose ability to estimate these things determines whether I make money or not, cannot give you a hard and fast answer. But I can give you a rough idea, based on jobs I've done with my own trained, experienced crew. You should probably double my figures to account for your own learning curve and to cover the time you'll spend purchasing materials and rounding up tools.

It takes my crew about 130 hours to install a simple, small (under 3,000 square feet), flat front yard with nice sandy soil. Nothing to pull out, just grading, irrigation, soil preparation, planting, and mulch. This time estimate wouldn't include retaining walls, steps, fancy pathways, or structures such as patios or decks. Reckon on adding about 70 hours if the yard is steeply sloped, or if the access is poor (as it is in most back yards). And figure on as many as 300 hours or even more if you have extensive existing landscaping to remove, lots of roots or rocks to contend with, or other unfavorable site conditions.

Don't forget, this is just the time it can take *skilled* craftsmen and women to do the actual work of making a garden. And we haven't even calculated the time you'll spend designing, or the inevitable time you'll spend running around for a three-quarter-inch slip fix to repair the pipe that just broke, or a new shovel to replace the one that just snapped.

Already discouraged? Don't be. One way to save time is to spend a little money. Even an accomplished do-it-yourselfer may want to consider using the services of professional contractors or designers for some parts of the landscape.

Hiring Pros

How do you decide which parts of your project to farm out to the pros, and which to take on yourself? Partly it will be a matter of understanding your own strengths, weaknesses, and tolerances. For example, if you have trouble keeping your ficus from death's door but can assemble a model airplane in just a few hours, you may want to do your own irrigation and have someone else do the planting. If trotting behind a loaded wheelbarrow gets your endorphins flowing, by all means don't let me stop you from doing all your own grading and soil prep. Have the aesthetic sensibility of a warthog? Then please, hire a designer . . .

The likelihood of needing professional help increases incrementally with the square footage of your yard. There is a big difference between installing a single drip line to water ten shrubs around a town home and setting up irrigation for a mixed half-acre of turf, xeriscaping, and roses. In general, any yard that's a third of an acre or more would probably benefit from the input of a professional (as well as from the use of power equipment, but more on that later).

The most technically confounding landscaping job is undoubtedly irrigation. All other things being equal, I urge you to consider getting a professional irrigation design, if not installation. Or, if not installation of the entire system, at least the construction of the mainline, valves, and wiring. At the *minimum*, run your own ideas by an irrigation designer, contractor, or qualified irrigation salesperson before proceeding.

Rough grading and drainage is my second choice of items to

have done professionally. It is sometimes hard for the unpracticed eye to perceive the subtle variations of topography that can make or break the drainage of a yard. Again, it may behoove you to simply hire an on-site consultant if all you need is technical expertise. A good consultant should be able to sketch or describe a couple of different solutions to your drainage woes. He or she should also help you determine the best way to grade your yard, given your particular design objectives.

Depending on what types of construction elements you'll include in your yard, you may want to consider hiring specialty contractors for items such as concrete patios and decks, especially if your own building skills range, like my own, from limited to nonexistent.

If you like working with your hands but lack an artistic eye, then a knowledgeable, creative designer can help. A talented landscape architect or designer may also be able to find design solutions to practical problems you thought were intractable. Or you may simply need a few preliminary sketches ("concept plans") to get you started down the right path. Again, you know your own talents or limitations.

The sections of this chapter that follow will help you select professionals who can work with you, not against you. But first, I want to tell you to be on the lookout for two things: credentials and references. There are plenty of wonderful people who don't have a clue about landscaping, yet manage to stay in business because they are just so darn *nice*. And then there are folks with degrees from Harvard and Yale, the presidents of worthy organizations and the recipients of numerous awards, who possess all the social skills of a praying mantis. The female one. Before you hire anyone, check their credentials and talk to previous clients.

Many homeowners are confused about the different terms used to describe professionals in the landscape field. What is the difference between a designer and an architect? Between a contractor and someone who does yard work?

First, let's break down these categories into their specialties. In the landscape field, there are people who design landscapes, people who install them, and people who take care of them. And sometimes one person or company will do all these things.

Landscape Designers and Landscape Architects

Let's begin with designers. All landscape architects are designers, but not all landscape designers are architects. "Landscape designer" is one of those meaningless terms like "karate white belt." We are *all* designers and white belts; there is no proficiency required for either designation. This does not mean that there aren't a lot of incredibly talented, creative, and knowledgeable designers out there. Some of the most wonderful gardens are created by people who don't have any formal schooling at all. Most designers, though, will have taken classes in horticulture or landscape architecture at two- or four-year colleges.

In California, landscape architects will always have a degree (B.S.L.A., B.L.A., or M.L.A.) in landscape architecture, as well as a license issued by the Department of Consumer Affairs. With the degree but no license, a "landscape architect" is just another designer. The licensing exam is grueling, with a very low pass rate. And in order to even qualify for it, a candidate must have a total of six years' combined education and approved work experience.

Many landscape architects don't do residential design. Landscape architecture is an eclectic profession, and includes city and regional planning and environmental restoration, as well as the more familiar specialty of garden design. Lots of landscape architects devote themselves to planning golf courses, freeway medians, urban plazas, or suburban shopping centers. So if you decide to use a landscape architect, you'll want to find one who specializes in home gardens.

Legally, the only thing landscape *designers* can do is planting design. In fact, according to the letter of the law, they can do planting design only if it doesn't affect "public health, safety, and welfare." But in reality, most of them also will do rough layouts of the paths, sitting areas, and other structural elements of a plan. By "rough layout," I mean that, for example, they will show where and how big an element like a deck is, but not its construction. If that same deck is designed by a landscape architect, the plan may show every bolt and beam.

What other distinctions are there between landscape designers and landscape architects? Well, cost, expertise, scope of services . . . Designers tend to charge less than architects, though this will not be true for all of them. In my experience, designers also tend to be more plant oriented (focused on "softscape"), while landscape architects are more, well, architectural. They excel at "hardscaping" features such as arbors and decks, road layouts and retaining walls, spatial organization and complex grading schemes. This is not to say that designers don't organize their plans spatially, or that architects don't know their plants. But in general, if all you need is a planting plan, I'd opt for a designer. If your house isn't even built yet, choose a landscape architect.

How do you find a good architect or designer? The obvious first step is to ask friends or acquaintances for their referrals. If you find one or two designers you think you could work with, the next step is to check out both their design blueprints and the (hopefully mature) landscapes installed from them.

Many nurseries will refer you to designers in your area. Such a referral can be a good resource because the designer will be familiar with local soils and microclimates, and will have his or her reputation (the source of continued referrals) on the line. But be wary of designer/nursery kickback or rebate schemes. Too many nurseries have poorly qualified in-house designers, or independent designers with whom they work closely, who will do free or rebated designs if you buy your plants at their establishment. I've come across several such plans, and they were deplorable: shade plants in full sun, plants with vastly different water needs grouped together, and so on. There may be some good nursery-affiliated designers, but a nursery's primary business is to sell plants. A good designer knows his or her worth, and charges accordingly, without rebates or freebies. Expect to pay from forty to sixty dollars an hour and up.

To find a good landscape architect, contact the American Society of Landscape Architects, at *www.asla.org*, and get a list of member referrals in your area. In general, membership in a professional organization will attract the leading practitioners of a given profession or trade, so this is a good place to start. You can find out more about the regulations concerning landscape architecture by contacting the regulatory agency for the profession, the Landscape Architects' Technical Committee, at *www.latc.dca.ca.gov* or 916-445-4954.

Expect to pay seventy to eighty dollars an hour and up for the services of a landscape architect. Most will use a formal contract, and will ask for a retainer or deposit before they begin work.

For both designers and architects, try to get an idea of the range of styles they feel comfortable with. Some designers have only one garden in them. They do the same scheme in virtually every landscape they plan. If you like a designer's style, and can be sure it will work with your site, your house, and your lifestyle, by all means use him or her. But I think you will be better served, in general, by working with a professional who designs in a variety of styles.

One last tip in working with designers (and architects): Beware the prima donnas with egos the size of Kansas. I don't care how well known they are, how many awards they've won or accolades they've received. If they won't listen to you (the garden dweller *and* the writer of their fine checks), they have no business doing residential design. A true artist considers client preferences as part of the mix of site conditions unique to each project.

Irrigation Designers

If you hire a licensed landscape or irrigation contractor to put in your sprinklers, you may not need a specific irrigation plan, since the proper functioning and longevity of the system will be their responsibility, not yours. In many cases the contractor will be able to design, bid, and install the system "on the ground." If many different stations are needed, however, most installers will charge separately to draw a design for your system on paper.

Do not use an unlicensed individual or company to put in your system. Chances are they won't know a whole lot more than you do, and as a consumer, you won't have any recourse once this becomes apparent. It may take weeks, months, or even years before shoddy workmanship or faulty hydraulic design becomes evident, and by then it's been a long time since your final check cleared the bank.

If you are installing your own irrigation, it may behoove you to get a professional irrigation plan, especially if yours is a large property (over a third of an acre to be landscaped). With a smaller yard, you may be able to do your own plan and then run it by the folks where you will be buying your parts to make sure it'll fly—or rather, flow. This will increase the chances that your system will actually work once you install it, and that water will be used as efficiently as possible.

Some landscape architects will do irrigation plans, but usually only as part of a plan for the whole yard. Many rely on the contractor who is installing the project to both design and install the irrigation properly and to code.

I would not recommend hiring either a landscape contractor or a designer to do an irrigation plan that you will install unless he or she is also a certified irrigation designer. Plain landscape designers are not legally allowed to design irrigation, only plantings, and contractors can legally design irrigation only if they install it themselves.

The best bet for the homeowner who wants to install his or her own irrigation is to use someone who is a Certified Irrigation

Designer. Certified irrigation designers know more than just how many gallons per minute a given head will draw; they are also familiar with the different water requirements of various soil and plant types. Ask your irrigation supply house, or contact the Irrigation Association at 1-703-536-7080 or *www.irrigation.org* for a list of Certified Irrigation Designers in your area. All other things being equal, I'd choose a designer who is a member of the association, because such a person is more likely to know about the latest products and techniques.

Contractors

Normally, you'll use a licensed contractor to install the parts of your landscaping you hire out, whether it is a general contractor to build your tool shed or a landscape contractor to do your irrigation mainline. I say normally because there are some instances in which you'd be better off another notch down on the totem pole of expertise. Some jobs are so small that it would be virtually impossible to find a licensed contractor who, with his additional burden of overhead, would be interested in taking them. Also, some jobs fall into the category of "yard work" rather than "landscaping." Examples of yard work are most activities involving hauling, mindless machinery operation, or excessive amounts of sweat: removing blackberries and poison oak, tilling the vegetable garden, weed-whacking a firebreak . . . Why pay Pavarotti to sing "Happy Birthday" to your one-year-old? And there do exist proficient, responsible craftsmen who lack contractor's licenses (though in this field, unlike the situation with designers, it is generally illegal to contract without a license).

Why choose a contractor who is licensed?

Well, first of all, it's the law. Any job costing over five hundred dollars requires that the operator be licensed. There are lots of ways to get around this, of course: time-and-materials arrangements, breaking jobs down into tiny increments. The more interesting question is: Why should you care? Especially if the guy who left the flier on your doorknob charges half as much as his legal competition?

Here's the worst-case scenario: You hire Whackenprune Tree Service to remove some trees. One falls onto your house, crushing their worker and your roof. Guess what? If Whackenprune isn't insured, you are responsible for all the medical care, rehabilitation, and disability of the injured employee, to say nothing of the repairs to your roof. Why? Because unlicensed contractors usually do not carry either Workmen's Compensation or liability insurance, which is why they can charge so little. Licensed contractors are required by law to carry these consumer protections.

Many people assume their contractor is licensed. By law, a licensed contractor must have his or her license number all over the place: on their stationery, their trucks, the ad in the yellow pages. If you don't see that license number, ask for it. Then do a little research to find out whether there are any complaints against the contractor. (In California, you can call the Contractor's State License Board at 1-800-321-2752, or visit their website at *www.cslb.ca.org*.) Licensed contractors can be every bit as scoundrelly as unlicensed ones; it's just easier to check them out before you hire them.

You should always ask for, and check, references. It astounds me how few people do this simple thing. Perhaps they feel it will jeopardize their budding relationship with the person to whom they are entrusting their project. Believe me, reputable contractors welcome reference checks, because they have nothing to hide. They also know their prospective client is about to hear an earful of good things about them. Call those references, and go look at the jobs. Are the details right? Look for clues to the overall quality of workmanship.

Make sure your contract is as detailed as it should be. Everything should be spelled out: quantities and sizes of materials, what work is and is not covered. Later, if there is any question, both you and the contractor can refer back to this document. It protects both of you from some of the ambiguities inherent in this type of work.

Never ask "When can you start?" Everyone wants to please, so chances are the contractor will tell you he can start soon, hoping to cinch the deal. And he may well do that. And then, a few days or weeks later, he'll go start another job, pleasing that client and leaving your project half-finished. It's not that contractors are evil wrongdoers, just that many of them don't know how to say "no" to their customers. You are much better off asking "When will the job be finished?" Your contract should specify both start *and* finish dates.

Never pay for much more than has been done to date. By law, a contractor cannot ask for more than 10 percent of the contract price or $1,000, whichever is less, as a deposit. Established contractors all have accounts where they buy their materials, so they shouldn't need money for materials up front. Progress payments should be broken down in such a way that you don't prepay for any phase of work not yet completed. And never, ever finish paying for a job that isn't finished. I'm not suggesting you act like a jerk, withholding money over trivialities like mud on a walkway. But you and the contractor should go over the scope of work and make sure he or she has done everything in an acceptable manner before you pay that last sum. Again, it's not that we contractors are any less honorable than the next person. We are just busy, and getting that last payment makes it too easy for us to cross you off our list and go on to the next job.

For any professional you bring on board, choose someone you feel comfortable with, that you can talk to, and with whom you have some rapport. There will be disputes, misunderstandings, and erroneous assumptions made by both parties. You can count on it. So choose a reasonable, fair person you feel you can trust. Don't be swayed by charming salespeople or flashy brochures. You want people who will stand and deliver.

Tree Services

If you will be bidding adieu to many trees, or even just one large tree, you will almost certainly want to use a tree service. Do not attempt to fell a big tree yourself unless you're tired of this life and are ready for the next. Tree work is expensive, and rightly so—you'd be shocked to see how much these companies pay in workmen's compensation and liability insurance. As I mentioned above, don't even *consider* using a company or individual without insurance; the hazards to life and limb, so to speak, are too great.

If all you need is tree removal, any company with proper insurance and licensing (a contractor's license) will do if its references check out, but if your trees need trimming, use an arborist certified by the I.S.A. (International Society of Arboriculture—see "Sources," at the back of the book). Yes, they're expensive, but bad pruning can permanently ruin the form and structure of a tree, often rendering it hazardous, and a mature tree is an irreplaceable treasure. Do not allow anyone to top or pollard a tree without very good cause. (A good arborist may refuse to do such amputations at all.)

Stump grinding is an added expense of tree removal. Unless you must plant another tree exactly where the old one was, or lower the grade where the tree was for a walkway or a patio, it probably won't be worth the cost to have your stumps ground down. Even if you do grind them, you will still have all those roots to contend with—and there really is no fix for *that* problem.

RULE NO. 2: SHOP SMART

The single best piece of advice I can give you about saving money on your landscape supplies is "Don't." Or rather, don't sacrifice the quality of certain key items, and don't skimp on materials if that results in more labor for yourself.

Resist the Lure of Freebies

Consider the example of the free plant. Perhaps your neighbor has made you the beneficiary of the mighty yucca tree he just extracted from his front yard. You hate to just throw it away, so there it goes, into the ground, next to the Japanese maple and the koi pond. First off, it will never look quite at home among its new companions. Second, did you ever wonder why your neighbor got rid of it? Do you really want to provide safe haven to the scourge that took him two full weekends to dig out and whose pups continue to haunt him? I'm a firm believer in adopting animals from the pound, but inappropriate or misbehaving plants are another matter entirely. Off to the dump they go!

Or maybe another neighbor has some rock she'd like to get rid of. True, it's that dreadful red lava rock, but hey, it's free, right? So you trundle down the street with your wheelbarrow and spend the better part of a pristine Saturday morning hauling forty dollars worth of dirty, ugly rock into your back yard, where it will be in the way of every landscape operation you perform before you can finally use it up. Isn't your time worth more than that for something that isn't really what you wanted anyway? Figure it this way: By doing your own landscaping, you are already saving lots and lots of money on labor. All that hard work deserves to be complemented with quality materials of your own choosing.

When in Rome: Shop Where the Pros Shop

If you want a professional-quality yard, you generally need to shop where the professionals shop. This is especially true for irrigation and low-voltage lighting parts. There is simply no comparison between the schlock sold at hardware and big-box stores and the good-quality supplies available where the contractors go. Plus, the people who work at these places can actually help you. They know more than just where to *find* that three-quarter-inch slip fix, they actually know what it is and how it works! Amazing! Invaluable!

It's not a bad idea to go to a landscape supply place (look under "landscaping equipment and supplies" in the yellow pages) before you begin your project, just to see what's out there in terms of bulk stuff you might want to use. This is where you'll buy your rock and your dirt, your mulches, and your amendments. And this is also where you can realize the biggest savings over the hardware stores' bagged products *and* actually sample a much greater selection of materials.

The one exception to my "Shop where the pros shop" rule applies to nurseries. First, wholesale nurseries don't want your business. No, really, they don't. They're not staffed to handle your horticultural questions, and more important, they don't want to undercut their "real" clients by selling to you, a lowly homeowner. So spare yourself the embarrassment of being shown the door, and instead develop a relationship with a good local retail nursery. They are set up to serve bright enquiring minds like your own; they can help you throughout the life of your garden as it matures; and they very much want your business. And, if you buy all your plants from them (see the section titled "How (and When) to Buy Plants" in Chapter 7), they will almost certainly give you a discount, bringing their prices closer to those of the wholesale outfits that don't want you.

RULE NO. 3: WORK SMARTER, NOT HARDER

Given the choice, I will always hire smart and scrawny over dull and brawny. Why? Because a smart fella can get just as much done in half the time as his stronger but less able-witted coworker, and do it better. A clever employee compensates for her diminutive size by lifting with her legs, using the correct tool for the job, and finding a shortcut into the back yard. Plus these folks are more interesting lunchtime conversationalists.

How can *you* work smart? Your mantra must be "efficiency." Here are a few simple tricks to save you time and energy when working outdoors. Be aware that our cultural prejudice against manual labor leads many people to dismiss as unskilled any work that uses the major muscle groups. Don't be fooled—there are tricks to even seemingly mindless tasks like shoveling dirt and digging trenches. I promise you, you will have a new respect for the work-booted workforce after you've walked a few miles in their shoes. (Or rather, boots.)

Clear the Decks

Before you begin, clear absolutely everything from the area you will be landscaping. This means all unwanted plants (and in some cases, even wanted plants, if they can be moved), trash cans, old pots, tarps, pieces of scrap lumber . . . If you neglect to do this simple housekeeping chore early on, it will interrupt the flow of work throughout the entire job. You'll have to stop the tiller to move the sheet of plywood leaning against the fence, and you'll chase the playhouse from one end of the yard to the other every time you trench or dig. Take stuff to the dump, or deposit it in an area where you won't be working, such as a patio. Understand that you will be disturbing the ground from fence line to fence line, and get that stuff *out*.

Move It Once and Only Once

This dictum applies not only to the junk already in your yard, but also to anything new you bring in. An object in motion should stay in motion until it can become an object at rest. So don't go fetch that lava rock from the neighbor till you have actually prepared a place for it to go. If you get it now, you'll move it again and again.

Most of the bulk materials you will buy have almost no value until they are where you want them. It is the labor expended in their delivery, application, and placement that gives them value. Take manure, for example. Stables can't *give* the stuff away, yet at the landscape place they charge you for it. Why? Because they can deliver it to your driveway! By the time you've schlepped that stuff into the garden, it is darn near priceless. Labor adds value.

Keep Tools in a Central Location

Find all the tools you'll need, and put them where they are easy to get to. If you have to root around in the garage every time you need something, you'll be more likely to limp along with the wrong tool than to "waste" time going and getting the right one. And it *is* a waste of your time to fetch tools one by one. This isn't the hokey-pokey we're dancing—saving steps is what it's all about.

Do One Thing at a Time

Stay focused on the task at hand. If you are grading, grade the *whole* yard. Completely finish one task before beginning another. There is a certain amount of setup time with physical work: finding the right tools, lining up your materials, figuring out the best technique, establishing a rhythm. If you jump from task to task, you'll lose momentum, and speed.

Don't Sweat the Clods

I know it's really, really hard, but don't rake up clods. I used to rake clods back when I first started doing this work. They just looked so *wrong* lying there. I couldn't have said what harm they caused, and I'll bet you can't either. So resist that impulse. Because what do you do with them once they're raked up? Why, then you must dispose of them. But you can't just take them to the dump, throwing away valuable topsoil, the end product of eons of eroding earth. Besides, it would take way too much time, money, and energy to load them up and haul them away. Do a quick cost-benefit analysis.

Instead, the thing to do with clods is to ignore them. It's true they're unsightly, but they really don't hurt anything, except our own (unrealistic) expectations of orderliness in the universe. Besides, the more you pursue them, the faster they breed. Get rid of all the clods while grading, and a whole new crop springs up after trenching. Dispose of those, and new ones appear as you plant. No, the only time you are allowed to rake up clods is when you are perfecting the finished grade for a lawn. And even then, it's usually better just to crush them down with a roller.

Do It Once, Do It Right

The corollary to this motto is "Hire a licensed contractor." At least if you hire someone and *they* screw up, you can rant and rave about them. But if you're doing the project yourself and *you* cut corners, then you'll have no one to blame but your own self. So avoid the dreaded tear-outs and re-dos, and spend the requisite time to do the job properly. It will cost you fewer of your three resources (time, money, energy) in the long run, and save you from the need to self-flagellate.

The Joy of Power Equipment

The older I get, the more I love power equipment. Why? Because manual labor, though noble and honorable and all, just *kills* me. My wrists have carpal tunnel, my shoulders get bursitis, and even my knees snap crackle and pop like breakfast cereal. So if there's a machine that can do a job, I use it.

What are your time and energy worth? Unless you earn the current minimum wage (and even my entry-level employees get double that), it will almost always pay to rent at least one essential piece of power equipment: the rototiller. And if you have room to maneuver it, especially if your soil is less than completely workable, you may also want to engage the services of a trencher. Dirt hard as a rock, even after soaking? Or, worse yet, dirt *is* rock? Consider a jackhammer (no, I'm not joking).

I am also a big fan of the power auger. I bought one several years ago and it paid for itself on the first job. In sandy soil, an auger can dig a five-gallon planting hole in, oh, say fifteen seconds. These four items—tiller, trencher, rotohammer (jack-hammer), and auger—are essential weapons in the arsenal of any serious landscaper. Of course, if there is a lot of clearing to be done, you may also want a weed-eater, a chainsaw, or even a brush cutter. And if you are doing serious construction work, there will be a whole gallery of fearsome tools to tempt you: backhoes and plate vibrators, tile cutters and nail guns.

Become familiar with what is available (most rental yards can hand you a price list) so that you can weigh costs against benefits as the need to rent arises. Once a tool is on the job, however, you'll find that it is downright indispensable. You'll use it for all manner of applications you never thought possible, and you'll weep copious tears when you must finally return it to its rightful home.

One more thing about power equipment: Don't forget the stuff you already have moldering away in the garage. Why pull weeds when you can mow them? Why cut blackberries with clippers when you are the proud owner of perfectly serviceable electric hedge trimmers?

I've gotten pretty creative. For example, I use my mower not just to cut grass in the summer but also to pick up and mulch leaves in the fall. In the winter, I mow down my ornamental grasses with it (and it spits them out as more mulch). Be creative, but don't be stupid. (You want to hear stupid? Back when I was a struggling gardener, we used to mow a steep hillside behind a convenience store by lowering a mower down it on a rope. One time it hit a nest of beer bottles, which exploded, flinging shards of glass far and wide. Luckily, I wear glasses . . .)

Do remember to call the Underground Service Alert at 800-642-2444 several days ahead of time if you need them to verify the location of underground utilities. Hitting a gas or water line with a shovel is one thing; doing it with power equipment is quite another.

RULE NO. 4: SAFETY FIRST

When I told my contractor friend Bob that I was writing this book, his first comment was "Tell them how to work safely!" So that's what this section is about—protecting yourself from yourself . . . as well as from the overzealous behavior of others.

The first key to surviving the landscaping of your yard is "Envision disaster." Learn to see danger, so you can head it off. Working with 300-pound boulders? What would happen if one got loose and rolled down that hill? Think like that.

The second thing to do is so obvious that it bears repeating. Read and follow safety instructions! Ever wonder why mowers, tillers, and their ilk have a "dead-man switch"? I don't think it was Madison Avenue's idea of a catchy marketing ploy. No, I suspect there are a few men who are actually, verifiably dead right now from the lack of just such safety devices. Don't be a dope and disable yours.

The third thing to do is to buy—and *use*—safety equipment. I never used to wear work gloves. And my hands always hurt, whether from an oozing blister or a bludgeoned thumb, an infected cut or a raw abrasion. Finally, at about thirty-five, I got smart, and now I wear gloves for everything but fancy needlework.

Don't work in sneakers, or, worse yet, flip-flops, golf shoes, high heels—you get the picture. I can't wear steel-toed boots because my feet are too wide for them to be bearable, but good leather hiking or work boots have always served me well. You need boots with thick soles and uppers to protect you from the exposed nails in the board you just stepped on, from bruising the sole of your foot as you bear down on the shovel, from crushing every bone in your foot when you do drop that boulder.

Use earplugs whenever you—or anyone near you—are operating power equipment, or you won't be able to hear your grandchildren singing "Happy Birthday" at your eightieth birthday party. Wear goggles or safety glasses when working with masonry so that even if you scorned that ear protection and can't hear those grandkids, you'll be able to read their cherubic little lips.

Lastly, learn how to spare your back. We humans were never really meant to walk upright. Nature likes to remind us of this from time to time by causing our backs to seize up in spasms of agony.

The sad news is that it's pretty much impossible to do landscaping work without risking back trouble. For example, a big back no-no is twisting and turning while carrying a load—a movement almost impossble to avoid if you're digging trenches or hauling rock. If you follow the pamphlets at the doctor's office, it could take you the better part of an afternoon to unload a couple of bags of ready-mix concrete. And forget shoveling dirt—following your doctor's guidelines would have you frozen from the waist up, moving from pile to wheelbarrow using only your feet, like a little toy soldier. But for your back's sake, do what you can to avoid or at least lessen this no-no twisting motion.

The one practice that *is* easy to adopt is to use your legs when lifting. After you get the hang of it, it is actually much easier to lift with your legs than your back, and you'll develop thighs like an R. Crumb beauty queen.

The key is to crouch down with your back straight and keep it that way, raising yourself by unbending your knees. What happens when you do this right is that you spend a lot of time with your butt in the air, looking foolish but enabling yourself to continue working long after all those other, hipper types are nursing their aching backs in the hot tub. Lifting with your knees is the *only* way to go if you are of the female persuasion, since upper body strength isn't our strong point.

A few final pointers: Hug heavy objects to your chest rather than holding them out at arm's length. Don't refuel a hot engine. Keep your yard free of tripping hazards such as rakes left upside down. And lastly, keep yourself well hydrated in warm weather.

I'll end with a brief discussion of a behavior I call "testosterone poisoning." We've all seen victims of hormonal excess peeling out at the dump, or wielding weighty sledgehammers overhead, or otherwise menacing civilized society. First off, let me assure you I have nothing against men. The doted-upon darling baby sister of four older brothers, I grew *up* with you guys. I *love* you guys. I'm just *afraid* of you.

The worst safety offenders, strangely enough, aren't the guys who work outdoors day in and day out. They've been hurt enough times on the job to have developed a healthy respect for tools, especially power ones. No, the most reckless guys are those who think manual labor doesn't take any brains, so they don't use *theirs* when doing it. Or they think physical strength is the answer to any problem. So, instead of outsmarting a dangerous machine like a tiller or trencher, they try to outmuscle it—often endangering not only themselves but anyone else unlucky enough to be nearby.

I remember when I lived in a commune (yes, it was a long time ago) and every summer we'd have a work party (an oxymoron if there ever was one) to get the garden in. We'd rent a tiller and the guys would take turns behind it as it bucked and leaped over the parched, hard dirt. If anyone had thought to soak the ground a few days prior to our yearly groundbreaking, our annual dance with death would have been a cakewalk.

The moral? Brains before brawn.

I hope these four Essential Rules—Plan Well; Shop Smart; Work Smarter, Not Harder; and Safety First—will help you get the most out of the chapters to follow and will save you needless physical (and fiscal) pain and suffering.

Chapter 2

Basic Landscape Design

Getting It All Down on Paper

I t can take just as much work to install an oh-hum yard as it does to put in one that'll stop traffic. Even the materials can cost as much for an uninspiring landscape as for a laudable one. Considering how many long hours you will toil, and how many large checks you will write, wouldn't it be nice to be rewarded with a garden commensurate with your efforts?

Good design is really just common sense. The only reason there is bad design is that most people don't take a moment to look critically at their own ideas. It is all too easy to become overly attached to the first idea that presents itself. (The worst mistakes of all, though, are made when people skip the design phase entirely and merrily begin hammering and shoveling without a plan at all.)

Here are just a few of the mistakes that I'd like to help you avoid. A little time spent at the drawing board will prevent you from committing these and many other needless landscape errors.

A LITTLE GALLERY OF DESIGN HORRORS

The Agoraphobic Path

This is the sidewalk that for some reason gets installed right up against the house, when there's plenty of room to be expansive.

Slinking along this path makes you feel as if perhaps the yard is not a safe place to be. In one variation, it's set away from the house just a foot or so, and in this scenario the planting area between path and house is so tiny that any plant unlucky enough to be placed there must be systematically and ruthlessly hacked, lest it block access.

The Path to Nowhere

This one is another old favorite of mine. It's usually quite a work of art. Great care has been taken in the selection of materials and in the workmanship. I've seen Arizona flagstone laid level and true, each piece placed with care and thought, with just the right matching shade of mortar between each slab. The stroller along this path is filled with a sense of anticipation and delight. And then the path ends. It just . . . ends. No bench, or pond, or even a loop back to the starting point. The disappointed stroller must do an about-face and go back along the same route whence he came. A good path is not an end in itself. It must take us somewhere. It should create, and then *fulfill*, a sense of anticipation.

The Unreachable Lawn

Yet another perplexing construction. This lawn is all you'd ever want: deep green and cool, an oasis from our concrete jungle. Except you can't get to it. The Unreachable Lawn is completely encircled with plants—which must then be tromped on or tiptoed through in order to gain access. Why go to all the trouble of creating and maintaining a lawn that can be seen but not enjoyed? You can't even get a mower onto this lawn, much less a toddler or a weary retiree. Like Odysseus's Sirens, the Unreachable Lawn calls out to us but never satisfies.

THAT FORM/FUNCTION THING: KNOW THYSELF

It is much easier to design a landscape you will love after you've lived with a few you didn't. My favorite clients are those who know what they do and don't want. They have endured a few poorly planned or even unplanned landscapes; they've labored over lavish lawns, pampered persnickety perennials, and shivered in the shade of overgrown evergreens. They nod knowingly when I tell them not to site the patio in the far corner (you will never use it, no matter how nice you make it).

The most common mistake people make when they begin to design is that they don't think about function. A well-landscaped yard is not just a collection of plants, or a mere decoration for the house. It is an experience shaped by a space. The quality of that experience is determined by how the space is formed. The intent of the yard, and its function, are more than the sum total of the materials used in its creation.

One concept that may help you understand this is to think of your garden spaces as outdoor rooms. Different parts of the yard will have different purposes: entertaining, reflection, play, and so on. The spaces, like rooms in a house, are defined by "floors" (lawn, patio, groundcovers), "walls" (plants, fences, and the like), and a "ceiling" (trees, arbors, and so forth). Of course, in an outdoor room, the walls may be implied rather than literal (a low hedge may separate one area from another), and the ceiling is sometimes only the sky and stars.

So the place to start in designing your yard is to think about what you need it to do for you. In some cases, it is just fine for a garden to be decoration; in others, it would be a tragic waste of valuable space.

It *is* often appropriate to treat the front yard as decor for the house, although this convention is increasingly challenged as prices for land escalate and lot sizes shrink. Because most front yards are viewed primarily from the street or entryway, they often act as a setting for the house. And since nearly all neighborhoods have restrictions on fencing for front yards, these spaces offer little of the privacy necessary for any purpose *other* than a decorative one.

Back yards are another matter. Most newer houses in California are designed with good links between the house and the back yard via sliding glass doors, French doors, and their relatives. Some houses also provide good garden access from one or more bedrooms. Even older homes have usually been remodeled to enhance the usability of the back yard. In addition, the back yard is usually viewed from the house looking out, so that the presence of the house itself becomes less dominant. Whereas the front

QUICK TIP

A good way to recapture the space in your front yard for private use is to plant shrubs that will act as a living screen, replacing the frowned-upon fence. If you plant on a raised earthen berm, the effect will be pronounced and more immediate. (See illustration below.)

yard should almost always be married to the architecture of the house, the back offers much more stylistic flexibility.

The function of the back yard will depend on a multitude of factors such as your lifestyle, your interests, and the time (or

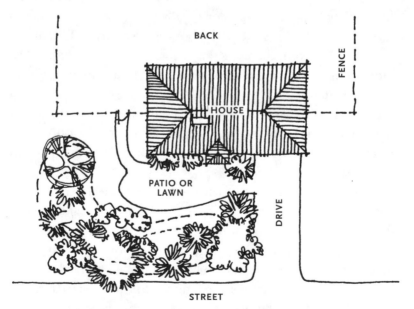

Recapturing the front yard with berms (dashed line) and plantings

budget) available for maintenance. If you love big parties, have more friends than a city councilman, and think any weekend is sufficient cause for celebration, you'll find a ten- by ten-foot deck off the family room a bit confining. If, on the other hand, you deplore all revelry and equate dancing and drinking right down there with playing cards with the devil, then why pour a patio big enough for a line of chorus girls?

Are you so obsessed with barbecuing that you grill even in the driving rain? Is composting a moral imperative for you? Is the view of the garden from the house more important than the experience of actually being out in the yard? Outdoorsy or indoorsy, get to know thyself. Plan for your passions, or your lack thereof.

Possibly the most important single factor to consider in designing your landscape is your parental status. One of the sorriest yards I was ever involved with was an absolutely pristine Japanese garden in which the play space allotted for the couple's five-year-old son was a barren, three- by three-foot, perfectly raked plot of sand. The rest of this immaculate yard was off limits. As a former child myself, I'd like to champion the cause of our heathen offspring. Every child needs a place to dig and tunnel, to create and destroy entire civilizations in the dirt. Make sure to leave some parts of your yard wild for a while, till your children tire of manipulating the earth to their own ends. It helps to think of the garden in terms of phases over time. The sandbox becomes a fountain; a lawn can later go where the play structure now sits . . .

Now that you've given thought to some of these issues, it's time to start making lists. Lists not only force you to take stock, they can reveal the existence of hidden assumptions. Go ahead and get the legal pad—we will be making lists to rival Santa's.

WANTS AND NEEDS

Your first list will show all the elements you think you Must Have (seating for six, lawn area for infant, greenhouse for orchid collection). The second list will contain all the things you Want to Have (lap pool, gazebo, koi pond with waterfall). Then, as you allot space in your preliminary sketches, you'll be able to see how much you can fit in (ideally, all your Must Haves and a couple of your Wants).

Here are some things I see in a lot of lists:

- *Sitting areas.* These include decks, patios, terraces, and the like. Use a tape measure to get some concept of how big a space you need. Allow for a barbecue, if that's your weakness.
- *Walkways and paths.* Put formal walks only where you really need them, as they tend to break up space. Designing paths and walkways is tricky. Because they strongly define spaces, their placement shouldn't be based one hundred percent on efficiency of movement from point A to point B. Yet, there is nothing more frustrating than being forced along an overly circuitous path when your destination is only a stone's throw away. You'll want to compromise between saving steps and the aesthetic concerns of delineating different parts of the garden.
- *Lawns.* Will these be for play or serve as the walkable green floor of an outdoor room?
- *Shade structures.* You could wait four to six years for a fast-growing tree to provide relief, or build an arbor and plant a wisteria or a grape, and have shade in just a couple of seasons.
- *Fencing.* Don't assume that the standard wood fence is your only option. If the view on the other side is nice, consider wire field fence (without the visually distracting top rail, if possible). There are even alternatives to the standard eight-foot deer fence, such as short double fences. Start noticing fences around your neighborhood, and go to a fencing company and see what options exist.
- *Seating.* Be aware that benches in the garden serve mostly to impart a leisurely ambience. Most people won't actually sit on one unless it is close at hand. But creating a welcoming

mood is as just as valid a goal as providing usable seating. So go ahead and buy that swan bench you saw last weekend . . .

- *Terracing and retaining walls.* Such structures are a necessity in steep yards, an optional enhancement in more gently sloping lots.
- *Swimming pools, hot tubs, and spas.* These are found more frequently in the Wants list than in the Must Haves list.
- *Storage and service areas.* Places to stash firewood, scrap lumber, the wheelbarrow with the flat tire, and the garbage cans. A dog run also belongs in this category.
- *Water features.* Ponds, fountains, waterfalls.
- *Garden structures.* Sheds, gazebos, playhouses, and so forth.
- *Play equipment.* Swing sets, sandboxes, sport courts.
- *Raised beds.* These are handy for vegetables and flowers, and in gopher country they're an absolute necessity.
- *Art or sculpture.* Such elements are nearly always considered a luxury, but in my opinion no garden is complete without the personal touch of a piece of art.
- *Outdoor lighting.* Sometimes a necessity, sometimes an enhancement.

STYLES, MOODS, AND THEMES

While you're thinking about how you will use your back yard and what physical elements you need to include, you should also be thinking about the feeling you want to create in different parts of the garden. For example, public spaces such as decks and patios off the living areas of the house are often open and spacious in feel, whereas a hot tub off the master bedroom may be intimate and enclosed. An imposing three-story house will want a grand, dramatic entryway; a bungalow set twenty feet from the sidewalk will require an entirely different approach.

It's a lot easier to detail the stuff we want in a yard than it is to define the mood we'd like to evoke. While the former is a list of items, the latter is defined in the play among these elements:

their size relative to one another and to a human, the materials used, the amount of detailing and definition of these materials, your plant palette, and myriad other factors.

Mood is partly the product of a landscape's type and style. Examples of different types of landscapes are formal and informal, symmetrical and asymmetrical; rectilinear, curvilinear, or any combination. Examples of different styles are Asian, Mediterranean, and Cottage Gardens. Have no idea what these terms mean? Here is a basic primer.

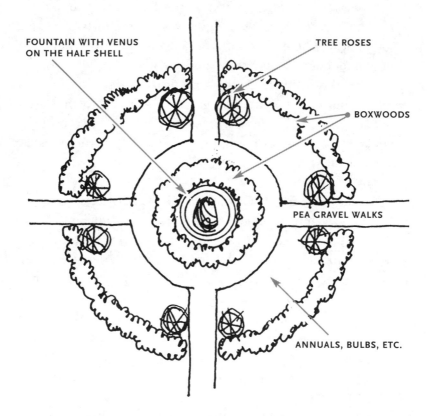

Formal garden

Formal Gardens

Most gardens are either formal or informal. Formal gardens are usually rectilinear (composed of straight lines rather than curving ones) and symmetrical (each side is a mirror image of the other); informal ones are curvilinear and asymmetrical. Formal gardens are typically associated with the great estates of nobility and the landed gentry. Think of rows of boxwood, straight lines along a strong central axis, and tightly controlled lines of sight. Areas devoted to roses, herbs, annuals, or bulbs are segregated by plant type and defined within tightly trimmed hedges. The natural form of an individual plant is often subjugated to the demands of the overall scheme, and many plants are heavily pruned to create idealized geometric shapes. Shrubs are clipped into hedges or made into topiaries; and trees are often pollarded (cut back to the trunk or a few scaffold branches), espaliered (trained flat), or even pleached (trained to grow into one another).

Formal gardens can be awe-inspiring and evoke a sense of grandeur, but they look most at home in front of, say, two-story houses with grand columns, set far off the street. In a word, estates. For most of us, even a double row of tree roses would look a bit pretentious, especially if your entryway is anything less than imposing.

Luckily, almost no one likes formal gardens anymore, at least not the traditional ones. Informal gardens are much more common—about 90 percent of the gardens I put in are informal.

Informal Gardens

Informal gardens are composed primarily of curving lines and are asymmetrical. The best example of an informal garden is the cottage garden, either the traditional English one or California style (same feel, different plants). Think meandering paths, small scale, intimate spaces, and an emphasis on the natural world over the man-made.

In truth, however, informal gardens can have as many design

problems as formal ones. The most common mistake I see is a failure to provide structure in the form of good "bones." For example, I've seen informal gardens with no trees or evergreens at all! The best informal gardens are carefully planned, and look as good in the winter, and years after installation, as they do that first spring.

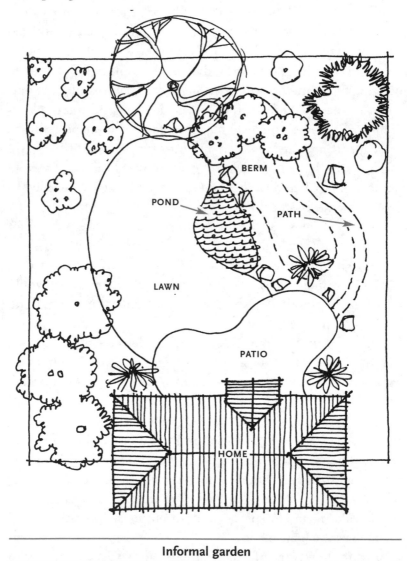

Informal garden

Neither Formal or Informal

Some garden styles resist being typecast as either formal or informal. Asian-inspired gardens are the best example. The forms of the plants are stylized and manipulated, yet the gardens themselves are flowing and asymmetrical. Landscapes based on a specific plant palette (natives, fragrant plants, or drought-tolerant plants, for example) can also defy categorization, since it is not the plants themselves so much as the way in which they are used that will characterize a garden as formal or informal.

Mediterranean-style gardens are another perplexing category. If you've ever been to that part of the world, you'll notice that the gardens there are very different from what we call a Mediterranean garden here in California. I've seen a lot of both public and private gardens in southern Europe that are nothing like the loose, billowy landscapes *we* describe as Mediterranean. For example, they really are formal gardens, usually laid out on a grid, with lots of gravel, oversized pots, and relatively few plants—a smattering of roses and culinary herbs, perhaps. It seems that what we like to call a Mediterranean garden here is really just a garden with a Mediterranean plant palette: olives and rosemary, lavender and grapes, and the like.

It's important to think about the architecture of your house when you're pondering which type or style of landscaping you will adopt—particularly, as I mentioned earlier, for the front

QUICK TIP

You don't need to nail down *precisely* what type of garden you'd like just yet. At this stage, all you need to be thinking about is what you might want. Start noticing gardens you are drawn to, and consider what adjective you might use to describe the feel of each. Observe how their spaces are defined, and the scale of the elements used to shape them. Start making lists of plants you like and those you don't like. Look at magazines such as *Fine Gardening, Horticulture,* and *Sunset* for ideas and inspiration, and start keeping a scrapbook of details that catch your eye.

yard. If you are considering a very specific look, such as an Asian-inspired or a formal garden, it won't hurt to do a bit of reading up first. Because such gardens historically have a very clear and well-defined purpose, it can be a mistake to treat them as mere decoration. For example, the intent of most private, residential Japanese gardens is to create an intimate space conducive to meditation and the contemplation of nature. This is why they are nearly always enclosed. So putting one in the front yard for all to see is really missing the point. Ditto with formal gardens, whose traditional purpose was to draw attention to their owner's great power and wealth, inspiring awe and envy on the part of the beholder. Which is why they inspire mirth (on my part, anyway) in front of any home more modest than Filoli.

SILK PURSES AND SOWS' EARS: IDENTIFYING YOUR ASSETS AND LIABILITIES

After you've named all the elements you want to include in your dream garden and have begun to think about what style or styles will work for you and your yard, you need to go on to your next list. This time, you need to objectively identify all the features, both good and bad, of your site. You can't begin to create a workable garden without first researching what you've got to work *with*.

We'll call all the positive attributes of your place "assets." The negative aspects we'll label "liabilities." This is no balance sheet, however: These two qualities rarely equal one another. Some sites are just a lot easier to work with. If you have a

QUICK TIP

Approach your inventory with a cool, critical, appraising, and yet opportunistic eye. It won't do any good to moon over pictures of shaded mansions in *House Beautiful* if the lone tree at your new home site is as big around as your thumb. On the other hand, if you have dead and dying trees, don't design your entire landscape around them. If the removal of trees—even healthy ones—will open up a breathtaking vista, then plan accordingly. Easily correctable liabilities should be *excluded*, and easily created assets *included* in your site inventory.

gorgeous old house, mature eighty-foot oaks, and a natural stream-fed pond on your site, your own improvements are almost negligible. If, on the other hand, you can manage to create a lush, peaceful oasis in the sterile side yard of your fixer-upper across the street from a refinery—well, now I'm impressed. (My big beef with gardening magazines is that they rarely represent the conditions under which most of us garden. So few of us *have* ten acres and a trust fund.)

Here are some examples of assets:

- *Pleasant views.* You may have just a single vista from the upstairs bathroom, or a sweeping panorama from almost every room in the house.
- *"Borrowed scenery."* Your neighbor's picturesquely rustic barn, or the open space behind your property.
- *Mature trees.* To qualify as assets, they must be of desirable species *and* in good health.
- *Desirable plantings.* The previous owner's collection of antique roses, or a nicely matured clump of rhododendrons.
- *Attractive architectural elements or hardscaping.* Your elegantly configured decking, your charmingly weathered brick patio, or your own *Architectural Digest* award–winning abode.
- *Serendipitous microclimates.* A sunny south wall under a generous overhang might provide a good spot to try plants that are not quite hardy in your area. A cold spot might be ideal for stone fruit.
- *Beautiful natural elements.* Boulders, desirable native vegetation, and their ilk.

Liabilities are any features that detract from the usability or beauty of the site. Sometimes an item will be both an asset and a liability. (Perhaps you love the swimming pool, but it requires fencing or expensive repairs.) Other times, the decision to place a given feature in one list or the other will be a matter of your own interpretation or taste. One person's lovely rustic barn is another's appalling eyesore.

Typical examples of factors that can have a negative effect on your landscaping efforts are the following:

- *Unpleasant views.* Your neighbor's six- by eight-foot "God Bless America" sign. Or even your neighbor himself.
- *Undesirable mature trees.* Despite their size, if they're in poor health or have insurmountable problems such as unacceptable litter or heaving roots, you'll probably want to get rid of them.
- *Problematic neighboring trees.* Trees next door aren't always a blessing. At my house, we can still have frost on our roof at 2 p.m. on a chill winter day. Why? Because the southern sun is blocked by our neighbor's towering conifers.
- *Unattractive architecture.* Either your own or your neighbor's.
- *Unfortunate microclimates.* A hot, treeless western exposure, or a cold, shaded northern one.
- *Existing features you'd love to get rid of.* The cracked but serviceable patio, the poorly designed deck you can't afford to replace, the ugly shed you need but abhor.
- *Steep slopes.* It is true that a sloping yard can offer a certain drama lacking in a flat site. In general, however, the expense of building retaining walls and steps and the absence of usable flat land for a lawn or a play area are more detrimental than beneficial.
- *Small or odd-shaped lots.* A very small lot can be a challenge to design if you must address several competing needs in a small space. Long, narrow lots, triangles, or other strangely shaped parcels all present unique challenges to the would-be designer.
- *An exposed, windy site.* Constant wind will drive you indoors on a sunny spring Saturday, curl the tender new growth on a Japanese maple, and cause trees to stoop like tired old women.
- *Poor soil conditions.* Pure sand, impervious clay, rocks.
- *Poor drainage.* Most problems are correctable, but your design may need to take severe drainage issues into account.
- *Pests (wild and domestic).* Not just deer and gophers, but even

our own kids and pets can restrict our design possibilities. Don't even *dream* of a nice koi pond if your dog has Lab or retriever blood in his veins.

- *Fire danger.* If you live in an area with steep, narrow, one-lane roads and lots of mature oily trees like eucalyptus and pines . . . remember the Oakland hills? Or, if you live in an area without fire hydrants (you should notice these things), a pool may be an insurance policy, not just an outdoor tanning salon.
- *Neighborhood restrictions.* CC&Rs (codes, covenants, and restrictions) and special ordinances may restrict the use of certain types of plants or mulches, tree heights, or the parking of boats and RVs.
- *Water restrictions.* Not just the ones we all endure here in the West, but specific local ones. In poor Marin County, the water bill can rival the tuition for the kids' academy. And some rural areas are served only by wells producing foul-smelling rust-colored sludge.

DRAWING YOUR BASE PLAN

Now that you've taken inventory of your site, it's time to make a scaled base plan, sometimes known as a "scaled drawing." What is this? It is a bird's-eye view of your property, done to a scale of, say, one inch equals eight feet, which shows all the salient features, good and bad, of your existing site.

What you need to end up with, by whatever means necessary, is a replica of your yard as it will be when you've removed everything that isn't going to remain. What you don't show (things that will be torn out) is just as important as what you do.

What Not to Show

The reason it's important *not* to show existing plants, walks, and such on your plan if there is even the possibility that they will be eliminated is that every existing feature remaining on the site will affect its design in some way. For example, even if you know intellectually that certain plants will be removed, it is still an eye-opening experience to see on paper what their elimination does for the yard. So be ruthless, and don't show any plant that can be transplanted or is not necessarily worth keeping.

Decide in the design phase what stays and what goes. When you see your property in the abstracted, bird's-eye view of your base plan, you can visualize how the disappearance of certain elements can create new opportunities. Deleting things like sheds, walkways, and trees on paper is a nice safe way to explore how their absence will affect things such as traffic flow and views in the finished landscape.

A short note here on demolition. Few people start their landscaping with a clean, new canvas. Most yards have unlovely vestigial artifacts that need to be purged. If there is a lot of stuff to take out, it may pay to hire someone to do the work for you, especially if you don't have a truck. It could cost as much to rent a dump truck or a dumpster yourself as it would to hire someone else to do both the clearing and the hauling. This is not skilled labor, however—look in your local classifieds under "Yard Work and Hauling." And don't let such yard workers even *touch* the trees you want to save. These are not professionals, and if you let them prune, you'll *want* the tree gone when they're done with it.

> **QUICK TIP**
> If you have the builder's or the architect's plans for your house, by all means use them (but check to make sure the house was really built as planned). You will still need to draw in things such as drives, trees, and walks, which may not have been included, but you will save a lot of time and confusing calculations if you have the house and its relation to the property.

What to Show

So what *do* you show? Here is what to include in your drawing.

The house! You need to show doors, windows, the garage, the driveway, and any decks or patios that are definitely going to stay. You do not need to show where the hose bib is, the PGE

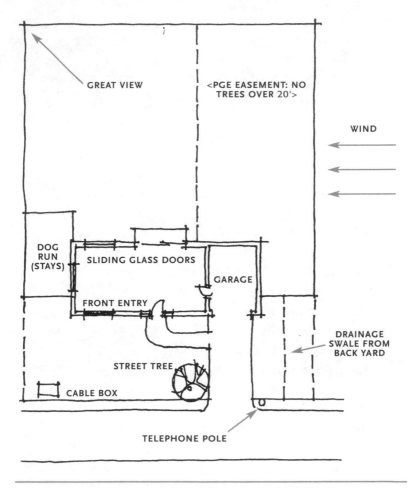

GREAT VIEW

<PGE EASEMENT: NO TREES OVER 20'>

WIND

DOG RUN (STAYS)

SLIDING GLASS DOORS

GARAGE

FRONT ENTRY

DRAINAGE SWALE FROM BACK YARD

STREET TREE

CABLE BOX

TELEPHONE POLE

Sample base plan with assets and liabilities

meter, or the downspouts. You do not need to indicate how high the deck is, or exactly how many inches wide the windows are. Really? Yes! Homeowners get all hung up on these trivial details, and they spend countless precious hours making sure their dimensions are true right down to the last millimeter. It's a horrendous waste of time—and furthermore, you'll end up with a plan so full of detail and tiny scribbled notes and dimension lines and arrows that there's no room to show what you actually want to put in.

The point is not that it's unimportant to know where your meter is. We all know that you don't want to plant a prickly pear in front of it. But give yourself some credit. Don't you already know where the meter is? Can't you trust yourself not to forget that fact when you're planting? Sure you can! Similarly, of course you need to know where your underground utilities are. But drawing them on your plan won't help you much when you're trenching—you'll want to draw them on the ground itself. The only "utilities" I routinely mark on base plans are septic lines, since you generally should limit the type of landscaping over them. Contact your county sanitation department for suggestions for leach fields.

Ditto with the inches thing. The

only time you need to consider inches in your measurements is for hardscape items (and not always even then). If you use expensive lumber that must be ordered and cut down to the last inch, yes, you should measure and calculate carefully. But for anything involving plants, or cubic yards of material, the difference between a bed that is five feet wide and one that is five feet three inches is negligible. So don't waste your time obsessing over it.

I usually start by measuring the house and then use it as a reference point to show the property lines. This relationship between the house and the property it sits on will be the most important information you'll need, for it will determine the dimensions of all the different yards: front, sides, and back. Once this has been done, it is easy to place items such as trees and patios in relation to those house and property lines.

Elements you need to show on the property as a whole are anything that will affect the basic design. These include most but not all of the items in your "assets and liabilities" inventory. If there are features on neighboring properties that have a big impact on yours (such as large trees), then include them, too. If you include too much detail (like every microclimate and boulder) you again run the risk of clogging the drawing up with information that detracts from, more than it adds to, your grasp of the overall space.

In Good Measure

It is important that your base plan be fairly true to reality, since you will use it to calculate the materials you will need as well as to apportion space for various activities in the garden. Begin by sketching the house as you see it, but in bird's-eye view. I just use a sheet of regular paper on a clipboard, with pencil and eraser. Don't worry too much about being in scale; just make sure every corner and bay window and landing is drawn in.

Then you can measure *each* item (door width, space between door and window, window, space between window and next window) separately, and add up all the measurements at the end. Or you can stretch a fifty-foot or hundred-foot tape along one whole side of the house and note each item (beginning of door, end of door, beginning of window, etc.) according to its

A GALLERY OF QUICK MEASURING TIPS

One: Buy a fifty- or one-hundred-foot tape if your place is bigger than average, or if your patience is anything less than saintlike. On really large places of a half-acre or more, it's easier to figure out precisely how many feet and inches your pace is, pace the whole property off, and then convert the number of paces to feet.

Two: Use a conventional scale, such as one inch equals four (or eight) feet, so that you can use a ruler in making your base plan.

Three: Make lots of copies once you've completed your plan so that you can freely scribble ideas and preliminary sketches on them.

point on the tape (2 feet, 4½ feet, 6½ feet, etc.). This latter, "baseline," method is much faster, and you can be certain the overall length of the house (the most important dimension) is correct. The incremental add-up system has potential for addition errors, and you can waste a lot of time checking your math. But if all you have is a twelve-foot tape, you won't have much choice.

Once you've got the house figured out, run a tape measure out from each corner, as if the side of the house

INCREMENTAL METHOD   BASELINE METHOD

WINDOW   3'   29'

4'   26'

22'

8'   14'

SLIDING GLASS DOORS   7½'

2'   6½'

WINDOW   2½'   4½'

2'   2'

0

Two different ways to measure

continued in a straight line until it hit the edge of the property. This is the distance between the house and the property line. Note this measurement for all the corners of the house, extending each side of the house at each corner. Now go ahead and draw in and then measure the fence lines or property boundaries (see illustration on next page).

Firming Up the Elements: The Base Plan

After you've finished taking your measurements, it's time to tally everything up and transfer your measurements and rough sketch to a more final form. So, if you haven't already done so,

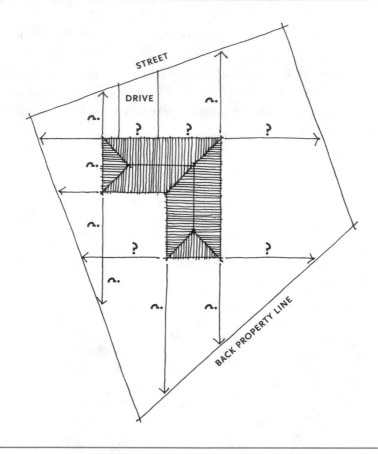

Extending lines from house to edge of property
Once you determine where these lines end on the boundary, you
should be able to "connect the dots" to draw in the property lines.
The most important dimensions to have correct are the house in
relation to these property lines.

head off to a drafting supply place and get a much bigger sheet
of vellum paper than you think you need. It is *so* frustrating to
spend a lot of time plotting the house, only to find that the
property line goes off the edge of the too-small piece of paper.
In fact, get *several* sheets of vellum, preferably at least twenty-
four by thirty-six inches, so you have plenty in reserve.

Get *gridded* vellum paper if they carry it. The grid (get it in
"eight scale") is very convenient for laying out right angles as

well as for a general reference. Another handy device to pick up at the drafting supply place is a rolling ruler. A rolling ruler ensures that all your lines are parallel to one another, so this is especially important if your paper has no grid. The only other fun gadget I'd recommend purchasing is called a flexible curve. It is useful for making curved lines, and, used at the scale of one to eight, it'll prevent you from making curves that would be out of proportion to the yard.

Now you have the fun task of trying to make sense of all those measurements you took. Don't be upset if they don't add up right—they never seem to the first time. And don't assume your yard is square. Sometimes, the reason side A is not as long as side B is because it just isn't. If your place doesn't look like the Winchester Mystery House when you get it plotted on paper, you are already way ahead of the game.

It is really important that you have the overall site drawing fairly true to reality. Go outside and double-check: "Yes, the yard really *does* get skinnier and skinnier at the end," or "No, the dining room is *not* in the neighbor's pool." The reason this is important is that everything you do will be based on these dimensions. So, if you are off by several thousand square feet, you could end up with miles of extra sod left over when you do the back lawn. An inch or two here and there won't break you (I round everything off to the nearest half-foot), but gross miscalculations will haunt you throughout every phase of the project.

Once you've got the house drawn correctly to scale and

positioned accurately as it sits on the property, you can heave a great sigh of relief, and celebrate by heading to the nearest Kinko's to make a few copies.

If all you *have* is a house and some fence lines, you should finish up at this point by showing where north is, noting the scale, and then making copies. You are done. However, if there is more to your lot than a house and fence lines, add the trees, shed, driveway, dog run, and whatever else to one of the copies you made. To place these secondary features in the yard, you should relate them either to the house or to the property line, whichever is closer or more convenient.

When there are a lot of indeterminate items like an entire grove of trees, I will often run my hundred-foot tape across the yard in two directions, at right angles to one another, plotting items in the yard according to their coordinates along each axis (remember X and Y from geometry?). It is usually easiest to make these X and Y (or "horizontal" and "vertical") lines by extending the lines of the house out into the yard. Perhaps the X axis is just the side of the house, and the Y line is the back.

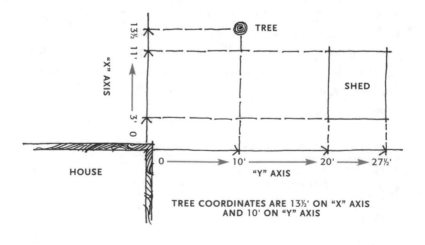

TREE COORDINATES ARE 13½' ON "X" AXIS
AND 10' ON "Y" AXIS

Baseline measuring using "X" and "Y" from corner of house

Shooting Grades

Sometimes you will need to know the exact elevation of a particular area of your yard in relation to another. For example, when you are figuring out the tread/riser ratio for a set of steps, you'll need to know how much "rise" (elevation) must be accomplished in the amount of "run"(linear distance) you have available. You will need to calculate elevational changes again when you build a retaining wall, to estimate the materials you'll need.

The low-tech way to shoot your grades is with a taut piece of string and a fifty-cent device called a "line level." Fix the piece of string to the ground at the higher of the two points whose height differential you want to measure, and stretch it tight to the lower point. Attach the line level and raise or lower the string until it is level. *Voilà!* The distance between the string and the lower level is the height difference between your high and low points. Mark it in tiny numbers on your base plan as a reference.

Once you've completed your measurements for all your secondary items, plot them on your original vellum paper base plan and then make more copies of this, your final base plan. This will be the base plan you'll use as a template for your subsequent landscape designing. You can now go on to make alternate base plans showing more detail, as described previously, should you want them.

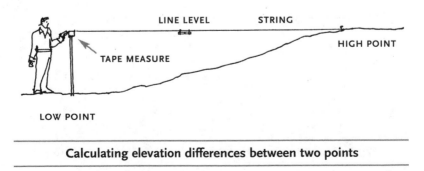

Calculating elevation differences between two points

Hurrah! You are now ready to do something a bit more creative. I'll bet you know your yard a lot better than when you started, though, don't you?

FUNCTIONAL "BUBBLE" DIAGRAMS

Once you have a good scale drawing of your yard, and a list of all the elements you'd like to include in it, lay a piece of tracing paper on top of the plan and find the biggest, dullest pencil in the house. Or a crayon. "Why a crayon?" you may well ask. Because I want you to resist the temptation of falling in love with the first idea that floats across your temporal lobes. If you only have a crayon, or the stub of a pencil from behind the sofa cushions, you won't be able to draw in each brick before you've had a chance to see if that's really even the right spot for the patio. You won't be able to show exactly where each four-inch groundcover plant goes before you've had a chance to explore different shapes for the planting bed. The stubby pencil or broken Crayola will keep you focused on what, where, and how big: the three most important considerations to resolve before you tackle any other design details.

What elements from your list of wants and needs are going to be in your yard, where will they go, and how big should they be? Let these be your only considerations at this stage of the game. Draw your chosen elements as loosely defined "bubbles," and worry about precise configurations later, once you've established their relative size and relationships to one another.

Begin by locating your sitting areas, the least flexible elements. Let me tell it to you straight: They are going to go right next to your back door/sliding glass doors/French doors. Why? Because we humans are lazy creatures. We cut across wet lawns when there is a lovely dry path only a few steps away, and we will not go and sit outside if we have to schlep our cool drink, wholesome snack, and trashy book more than a half-dozen steps. We think we will, and our intentions are good, but the fact is, we won't.

By the same token, if you put a gazebo in the corner of your yard, feeling certain you'll be out there to admire the view from it on fine summer evenings, be forewarned. The only view you are likely to admire is the view of your fine gazebo, from the nice deck so conveniently located just off the kitchen. Oh, sure, you'll go out there right after you've finished building it. That first week.

Next to my pond I have a very cool looking bench shaped like a pig. If I am very stealthy, I can sneak up onto it and spy the bullfrogs dangling in the water with only their eyes above the surface. But do I ever sit on my piggy bench? No, I do not. The steps off the nearby deck are closer to the house, and they're shady, too. But I enjoy the view of the bench from the bedroom, and that is enough.

So the deck/patio goes right off one or more of your outdoor access points. How big should it be? Let me tell you, you have a big advantage over any designer you could hire in that you can always step outside during the design process and verify your assumptions or test your theories. Plus, you are your own best customer. You don't have to try to explain what it is you want—you can just draw it. So go outside, and mark off about where you'd like your sitting area to go. People are remarkably good at this, even folks with no training in design or spatial thinking at all. Yet surprisingly few do this little reality check. It is all too easy to start drawing and never look back.

Once you've marked off your proposed sitting area, take some measurements to get an idea of the size. You don't need to figure out the *exact*

shape or size, all you need at this stage is a rough approxima-
tion. Your margin of error can be within two or three feet for an
average yard, more for a big place.

After you've drawn in the approximate location and dimensions of your primary seating area, you can begin plotting the
other elements you want to have. (Hold off on the walkways,
though, until you have your destinations in place.) I suggest at
this juncture that you locate all the things you'd like to have on
paper before "editing" your efforts by verifying them outdoors.
Right now, your job is to generate ideas. You can cull them later.

WHAT GOES WHERE

It's time to think "outside the box." Just because you've always
had the garbage cans next to the garage, is that really the best
place for them? Could the vegetable garden be moved to a sun-
nier spot? You will never be as unencumbered as you are right
now, with a (relatively) blank piece of paper and an endless array
of possibilities to explore. So open yourself up to your yard's
hidden potential, keeping in mind just a few pointers:

- Shade structures will most likely be located in conjunction
  with seating areas, though sometimes you'll want to provide a
  covered walkway, particularly where summers are hot.
- The function of turf areas (to provide a green respite for the
  eye, or a play area for children) usually dictates that they be
  placed just off the major sitting areas. A grassy area tucked
  away out of sight can be a welcome surprise along a path, but
  it won't get as much use as one that is visible from the house.
- The location of terracing and retaining walls will be dictated
  by your need for flat space as well as by the topography of
  your site. If you plan a terrace or a retaining wall, you will
  need to figure out the elevation differences between key
  points in the yard (see the section "Shooting Grades," on
  page 46). Be aware that in most localities any retaining wall
  over three feet high requires a permit. In addition, the engi-
  neering logistics of high walls can be daunting; you are often

better off terracing your slope to create two lower walls than
retaining the soil in one higher wall.

- Always locate a swimming pool where it gets the maximum
  amount of sun. That seems obvious, but sometimes aesthetic
  considerations override this practical one. You won't want to
  swim in a cold pool, no matter how lovely the reflection of
  the tree overhead. Speaking of trees: Avoid siting your pool
  near large trees, or planting large trees near your pool. And
  don't be fooled into thinking that evergreen trees are less
  messy than deciduous ones. They just drop leaves or needles
  all year, instead of over a couple of months.

- You may want secondary sitting areas off a master bedroom
  or a front entryway. These are usually smaller, more intimate
  spaces than the public spaces used for entertaining or family
  gatherings.

- A built-in barbecue, or even just a designated barbecue spot,
  should be located near the outdoor access point, but ideally
  not in a highly visible location. While subscribers to *The Grill
  Out Times* (yes, there really is such a publication) may dis-
  agree, a Weber does not a fine focal point make. On the other
  hand, a barbecue devotee shouldn't be outright excommuni-
  cated on account of his (and I think that *is* the operative pro-
  noun) vice. Particularly at parties, others of his kind will seek
  him out, creating festivities hopelessly split along gender
  lines.

- Hot tubs are like sitting areas; if you put one too far from the
  house, you simply won't use it. Honest. You also want to
  make sure you provide some sense of protection from prying
  eyes. Hot tubs seem to work best just off the master bedroom, with at least one side up against the house. We humans
  like to sit with our backs protected.

- Speaking of which, garden seats should be placed along
  paths, under an overhead shelter (a tree canopy will do
  nicely), with their backs against something (the trunk of the
  tree, or a fence). Again, this has to do with our primeval

past—we like to sit at the edge of the forest, looking out onto the savannah.

- Situate water features where you will get the maximum pleasure from them, usually near the house. I like to make sure they are visible from at least one room inside the house, where they'll lure someone outside. A pond or a fountain is a powerful focal point, so give some thought to its placement. One trick is to put it where the eye goes. Oh, you never noticed where your eye goes? Step outside the house and look out. Where is the first place your gaze lands? That may be a good spot for a water feature—or some other riveting item, such as a piece of sculpture, or a huge boulder, or even a piggy bench. (Almost anything that is not a plant can serve as a focal point. Plants, even the most bizarre and unusual ones, tend to blend in, rather than catch and hold the eye.)

- Vegetable gardens follow the pool rule: maximum sun, away from large trees. It is nice if they can also be hidden from view, since for many months of the year they may be less than totally attractive. A more structured vegetable garden, with permanent paths and perhaps raised beds, always looks neater, even when vacant, than the odd patch of designated dirt.

- The "edible garden" approach is one way to avoid the vegetable garden ghetto, but it can be tricky to accommodate certain plants in an established garden. Any plant like corn, capable of growing from kernel to King Kong in a couple of months, is perhaps better off by itself. Edible gardens, in my opinion, work best with perennial crops like rhubarb, asparagus, berries, and herbs, where you don't have to deal with the differing water requirements between newly planted annuals and established perennials.

- Play equipment for young children should be situated where it is visible from the house so that the child-watcher can multitask if he or she chooses. Though it's true that most play equipment is unspeakably ugly, and probably the last thing you want to see from your elegant dining room, you should still let practical considerations override aesthetic ones in this instance. Figure it this way: The kids will outgrow the stuff just about the time you don't even notice it out there anymore.

- Storage areas and dog runs should go where they are not visible from key spots like the house and sitting areas. Often the side yard is the best spot, especially as most dogs don't like being any further from their people than necessary. Nothing is sadder than a dog in a run all by himself up against the back fence. You are unlikely to walk all the way out there to say hi, and Woofy knows it.

- The purpose of garden structures will dictate their placement. For instance, the logical spot for a potting shed would be near the vegetable beds or the cutting garden, while a playhouse can be nearly anywhere. (Unless it's one of those especially hideous orange plastic ones, in which case get it out of view. Please!) A pump house needs to go over the pump, and the gazebo needs to go as far away from the house as possible. Right? (Actually, I *like* putting gazebos off in the distance. They are great focal points. Just don't expect anyone to actually use them, except for the occasional wedding ceremony.)

- The design of any garden structure (buildings in particular) should be carefully considered. In some cases, you will want to match the architecture and colors of your house; in others, you can add a sense of whimsy or elegance currently lacking. If you must settle for unattractive ones, like one of those ready-made sheds with the hipped roof, that's okay. Just hide it. The homeliest edifice around is no match for a thriving Cécile Brunner rose.

PATHS AND WALKS

When you think you've put in all the things you'd like, or can fit in, give some thought to your walkways. Access and circulation are a crucial part of any landscape.

You should begin by distinguishing major paths from minor ones. Gaze into your crystal ball and envision your travel patterns in your yard-to-be. Is there a beaten path between the vegetable garden and the back door? Between the garage and the dog run? These are your major paths and should be wide—at least three feet—level, and clearly designated. (Other, minor paths may not even need to be called out as such; if you need to travel a given route only a couple of times a year, a simple opening in the plantings may work better than a concrete walkway.)

In the front yard, the standard path from driveway to front door tends to overemphasize the driveway, and it doesn't serve those who park on the street. To make the front yard appear more welcoming and to draw attention to the entryway, provide an additional walkway from the street to the front door. This and the route from the drive will be your major paths. You should be able to walk on these paths without thinking about your footing, so smooth paving is usually the best choice. (Think about your liability. Anyone, bosom buddy or litigious enemy, can tread these routes.)

In side and back yards, I usually provide a hard-surfaced walkway from one side to the other, connecting important sitting areas and frequent destinations. Your choice of materials will be dictated by how much and what type of traffic you need to accommodate. For example, a cunning stepping-stone path down a side yard can be a real bummer if you have to haul a lawnmower across it.

Secondary circulation in the back yard can be as simple as access through the plantings. Particularly where you do not want to draw attention to a passage or destination, this is frequently the best solution for rarely frequented routes.

Paths *can* serve primarily a decorative purpose, but remember my caveat at the beginning of this chapter, and provide a credible destination for them. Though the experience of the path may be the point, the human mind still insists upon having its expectations of the universe fulfilled. Paths are supposed to go somewhere, so don't disappoint.

"But what about plants?" you may well be asking. "Aren't they what a garden is all about?"

Funny you should ask. I am a hopeless plant nut. Nothing fills me with more delight than a new find at the nursery. So it may seem strange for me to advise you to hold off on thinking much about your plantings at this stage of your plan. At this point, plants are just a means to an end. Draw in a generic-looking tree where you need to hide the telephone pole, or where you know you'll want shade, and put in a cartoonish hedge where you want to screen the pool from the nosy neighbor boy. But hold off on any real planting design until you know what areas will be designated for plants and until you have committed to a particular style or theme for the garden.

Once you've come up with a diagram showing the location and size of the various things you'd like to have in your yard, you may put down your stubby pencil or crayon end. Take the drawing and set it aside where you won't see it. Cover your base plan with a fresh sheet of tracing paper and go do something else for a while.

Then later—perhaps even several days later—return to your base plan, take up your stumpy writing implement once more, and do another bubble diagram. Do not look at or even think about your first drawing. You want to come up with new ideas, not admire your original ones.

The point is to explore possibilities that might have escaped your attention the first time around. When I am doing these sketches, I force myself to do several even when I am quite pleased with the first. A sketch just takes a few minutes, and can end up saving you a real headache, or sparing you from one of

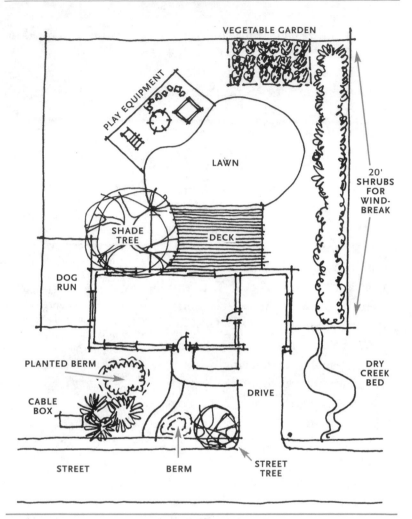

Sample bubble diagram

those design embarrassments we *didn't* mention at the beginning of the chapter.

REFINE YOUR IDEAS

It is now time to sort through your ideas and harvest only the finest and fattest fruits of your labors. Look through your drawings, show them to others, walk through your ideas in the yard, and begin to weed out the weaker elements in each. I usually find that one sketch will stand out as best, while I may adopt some selected features from the others.

When you think you've got the germ of a plan on paper, go lay it out in the yard, using flags and paint (see Quick Tip on this page).

Since you are still working with rough sketches, you don't need to be terribly accurate or precise. All you want to do is lay out your plan in enough detail to be able to visualize the finished result, and to walk through the yard and see how the circulation works. This is such an important thing to do! You still haven't spent any money on materials, or burned any calories behind a shovel. Often, a scheme that looks great on paper can fail dismally in this preliminary walk-through.

QUICK TIP

Use different colored flags to denote different items. The patio is yellow, the shed is orange, the lawn is white, and so on. To lay out curves, use your garden hose and then mark its place with chalk, flour, or marking paint. What's good about using the hose is that it prevents you from making a lot of little squiggly lines, a common beginner's error when using curves in the landscape.

Walk out to the imaginary vegetable garden. Is the path wide enough for a wheelbarrow? Once you're out there, you'll need a hoe, won't you? If you have to go get one from the garage, is that going to be a big pain? Maybe you *do* need a tool shed near that garden.

Go back in the house and look out the living room window. Will the arbor obscure the view of the mountains? Will you be able to see the waterfall from the sofa, or only from in front of the fireplace? Go to the spot where you've drawn the deck. Will it be so high off the ground that you can see into the neighbor's windows? Maybe a patio, dropped down a few feet to ground level, is a better idea. And that landing for the patio: Is it big enough so you don't feel as though you're going to be pushed off it by someone coming along behind you?

These are all questions you should be asking (and answering) now, while the world is still your oyster. Once you have installed something, its placement will dictate what comes after, and you will have lost the complete, invaluable flexibility you have right now.

Another thing to check at this stage is the overall balance of your scheme. For example, items with a lot of visual weight should not be clustered all together in one quadrant. You wouldn't want to put the pergola and the pool and the changing room and the granny unit all on one side of the back yard, leaving the other side an empty expanse of lawn. And you wouldn't want to place a big obstacle, like a freestanding fountain, right in front of your entryway. (Do we really need to study *feng shui* to figure this out?)

Once the bones of your landscape have been worked out, modify your drawing as needed. Next you can begin to refine

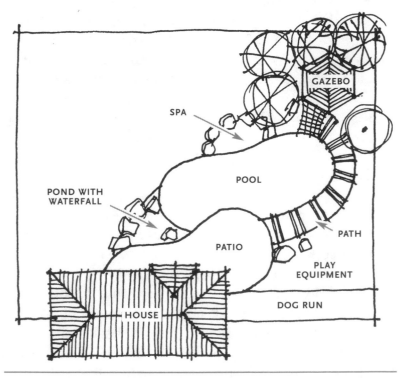

Unbalanced landscape

your plan. Congratulations! You may now move on to what most people think of as the fun part.

It's time to think again about the mood, the feel, and the style of the garden (the type—formal or informal—will likely have already been dictated by the layout of your sketch). If you want the Mediterranean look, for example, you'll be choosing warm colors and materials like terra-cotta and decomposed granite over brick and slate. Items like birdbaths and benches should also relate to your chosen style. A rustic garden with dry-stacked stone walls, a split-rail fence, and railroad-tie steps is not the right place for that shiny steel sculpture shaped like a corkscrew you admired at the Home and Garden Show.

SOME RULES OF GOOD DESIGN

The first rule of good design is "Be consistent." Actually, I've already alluded to this many times in this chapter. Landscaping in front should relate to the house; a rustic garden brooks no steel corkscrews, and so on. Another way to phrase this is "Be disciplined." You can't include everything in one yard. So, even if you love palm trees, don't put one in your Japanese garden. Very good designers can get away with this sort of thing and make it look whimsical and brilliant. But don't count on being able to pull it off yourself unless you're a true artist. And even then . . .

The second rule is "Repeat." Don't put just one big boulder in a yard. Put in a cluster of three or four, and then a couple more groupings a little further on. Make the retaining wall of the same stone, instead of lumber, and consider edging the gravel path in that same stone, as well. Right?

My last rule is "Contrast." If all your hardscape is the same dull brown of faded redwood, and your plants are all the same predictable shade of Crayola grass green, you will quickly bore your viewer. Create contrasts even as you repeat and harmonize. Even within a cohesive color scheme, one based on the warm apricots and tans of Mexican tile and flagstone, for

QUICK TIP

It's fine to pore over magazines and those garden books with the glossy photographs, but balance your perusal with trips to local supply houses to check on the availability and price of the materials you're drawn to. It won't do you much good to fall in love with Connecticut bluestone if it has to be trucked over long distances (like, from Connecticut), making its cost prohibitive. Plus, you might decide you're not as crazy about Arizona flagstone as you thought, when you see how much it costs. Pea gravel starts looking better and better.

example, provide a few spots of intense or opposing color—say a cobalt fountain, or a purple gate.

Contrast your forms and textures as well. Imagine a garden where everything was tall and skinny: Italian cypresses and flagpoles and Ionic columns and . . . palm trees. A few low rounded forms would be a relief, and would make the tall skinny things really stand out in comparison. Gray-foliaged plants will make the green ones next to them look that much greener, and soft fuzzy lambs' ears will emphasize the coarse nubbly grain of rough, uncut stone.

I could go on and on about design principles. But we're aiming for Grandma Moses here, not Leonardo da Vinci. Some of the most charming yards I've known were designed and installed by regular homeowners with good instincts, a passion for plants, and the willingness to rectify their mistakes.

How do you know when your design is done? Well, a design, like a garden, is never really done. Each action you take will result in an equal and opposite reaction. Once you get the retaining walls drawn in, you may realize that a much better spot for the lawn is below the house, not above it as you had planned. That's fine; you made the plan, and you can change it. It is so important not to be too married to your own ideas, your mistaken assumptions and preconceived notions. Save marriage for your spouse! I always change my plans as I install them, and it is always for the better.

I still haven't given you permission to use the ruler, the flexible curve, the compass, and the drafting pencil you so eagerly bought. Here's my advice: Don't design anything in detail till you are pretty close to building it. This is because you could invest a whole lot of time doing painstaking drawings and then, when you're finally ready to implement them, find that everything has changed. So stay loose, if you can, till you actually do need to know precisely how much lumber, how many square feet of sod, and how many pallets of stone you'll need.

Ditto with the planting plan. Have some idea of what you want, and be gathering lists of things you like, but don't bother actually counting how many four-inch potted perennials you'll need until you're ready to order them. Because planting is one of the last things you do, it seems to get shifted around the most of all. After you build your studio, you may realize that it screens the neighbor's junkyard just fine and you won't need to plant that photinia hedge after all. Or on paper, it looked as though there would be plenty of room for a giant sequoia next to the swing set, but now that you have opted for the deluxe model you'll be lucky to fit in a pompom juniper.

Speaking of planting design, I suppose it *is* time.

OUR LEAFY FRIENDS

Even though I know the names of thousands of plants, when I am asked, "What plant should I put here?" I am always at a loss for words. "Let me go back to my office," I mumble, "and I'll get back to you." I never know just the right plant until I spot it in one of my many plant lists. I have lists of deerproof plants, plants that are fragrant, plants with foliage golden and gray. I have lists of heritage plants, poisonous plants, plants for use in fire country, and plants that tolerate wind, poor drainage, and drought. I know plants that'll do everything but set the table.

The plant lists you use will, of course, depend on the style of garden you ultimately adopt. My favorite source, after all these years, is still the *Sunset Western Garden Book* (referred to as "the Bible" by those who depend upon it in their line of work). With each new edition, the "Plant Selection Guide" gets better and more exhaustive.

Your local UC Master Gardeners' desk (see "Sources" at the back of this book) will have good lists, too, some screened for hardiness in the counties they serve. Sometimes the horticulture department at your local junior college will offer plant identification classes geared to your region. But check first—not all classes are regional. For example, a plant ID class meant as a prerequisite for a four-year degree in landscape architecture includes plants from a broad geographical area. You should always check any plant you decide to use, from whatever source, in the *Western Garden Book* to make sure it fits your needs and site conditions. In fact, I would recommend taking "the Bible" along with you on those inspirational trips to the nursery. That way, if you see a plant you simply must have, you can look it up to make sure all its characteristics (for example, it may attract aphids or be poisonous to small children) are ones you want to live with.

> **QUICK TIP**
>
> Resist the urge to buy a single plant until you are completely ready to begin planting (and this, my friends, is a very long ways away). If you give in at this point to the siren calls of the gorgeous rose in full bloom, the perfectly formed Japanese maple, or the sale on dahlia bulbs, you will be lucky—and an exceptional horticulturist indeed—if they are still fit to plant by planting time. A much better strategy is to visit nurseries regularly throughout the year and make notes of the lovelies that catch your eye. (I'll allow you to buy a few annuals to grow in pots, to take the edge off your craving.)

I must warn you to ignore plant recommendations in any gardening book intended for a widespread audience. What grows well in Indiana, New Jersey, or Wales may fail miserably here in Northern California. Stick to books written, at the very least, for the Western states. Glean ideas from the others, if you must, but when they talk about how easy tree peonies are to grow, or how vigorous and floriferous lilacs are, just turn that page.

If your garden theme *is* the plants you will use—for example, if yours is to be a garden featuring California natives, or plants that provide bird habitat—then your plant selection task is vastly simplified. You will still have more plants to research than you will know what to do with, so don't despair about limiting the possibilities for creating something special and unique. Limiting choices is a *good* thing in planting design!

Horticultural Considerations

It is crucial to know the projected height and width of your selected plants at their maturity. Most people think a "low-maintenance landscape" means one with no lawn and lots of mulch. But in my experience, it is the *type* of maintenance you'll have to perform that matters. And nothing is more thankless than having to hack away repeatedly at a shrub that yearns to be eight feet tall, growing with wild abandon under a four-foot window. Select plants that will fit their chosen spot. I know it's hard to visualize that cute little houseplant-sized Christmas tree becoming eighty feet tall. But believe. Believe. The fortunes of tree companies far and wide thrive on the tenderhearted mercies of plant lovers like you.

Another critical mistake is to think you can force a plant to grow where it's not adapted. The plants always win. They'll die on you, just to prove their point. Get to know your yard well—its microclimates, and the path of the sun as it travels across the sky, especially in the summer months. Take note of north- and east-facing exposures against the side of a house or under a mature tree, where it's shady. Sometimes people make the mistake of assuming that because a spot is always shaded when they normally see it (before they leave for work in the morning and when they come home in the evening), it is protected all day. In the hours between ten in the morning and three in the afternoon the sun is at its most intense and will scorch the tender leaves of shade lovers like hydrangeas and rhododendrons.

By the same token, make sure you don't force a sun worshipper such as rockrose or lavender to languish in a spot with anything less than full, dawn-to-dusk sunshine. Most sun lovers will survive in the shade, but they become grotesquely attenuated as they reach for the vital rays, and they bloom sorrowfully if at all.

Another word to the wise: Avoid short-lived plants. Ever wonder why certain plants look so ratty after a while? *Euryops*, lavender, *Erisimum*, *Lavatera*, and some species of *Ceanothus* all die tragically young—or, if they survive, they'll look so leggy and miserable you'll consider a mercy killing via the shovel. If you simply must have such plants, use them sparingly, and understand that they will need replacing every few years. Or use them intentionally as quick fillers while you wait for more desirable, longer-lived species to mature. You can even use this trick with trees, but make sure you'll have the discipline to remove the fast-growing, short-lived "bad" trees when they begin to interfere with your slower-growing "good" ones. Using fruitless mulberry for some quick shade, or Leyland cypress as an expedient windbreak, is just fine if you're up to murdering them in the prime of their life.

Let's begin designing your plantings by using your refined hardscape drawing as a template (make copies of this document, so you can scribble away on them freely) and drawing in the plants that will serve a clear, specific purpose. Start with the largest plants, and work your way toward the smallest ones.

Trees First

In many yards, trees are used singly, as specimens. Of course, in really large gardens or country properties, there is nothing grander than a double row of liquidambars down the driveway, or a majestic line of poplars off in the distance. But most urban and suburban gardens will have limited space and conflicting needs, necessitating a more restrained approach.

If you don't already have them, draw in large deciduous trees to shade a western or southern exposure from the hot afternoon sun, unless you live where any sun at all is a cause for dancing in the streets. Then perhaps you need an evergreen tree about twenty feet high to hide the house across the way, and maybe you want a small specimen tree in the side yard between your window and your neighbor's. Once you've determined the desirable height, width, and shape of your trees (some are columnar, some shaped like lollipops) and whether they should be evergreen or deciduous, you can choose likely candidates from your list(s).

Spend a long time selecting your trees. The right tree can enhance your garden for years to come and add thousands of dollars to the value of your house. The wrong tree can be a real curse. When we first moved to the house where we have lived now for ten years, there were only three trees: an oak (which we still love), a weeping willow (which we loved dearly but which perished), and a sycamore (which we barely noticed). It wasn't until that sycamore got really big, and I had an entire shade-based garden in place beneath it, that it started to provoke my ill will.

In the fall, the leaves drop, and that's fine. But they never, ever break down. My inclination is to let falling leaves rot where they land, but sycamore leaves appear to be treated with preservatives, they last so long. Then this year, the mighty beast developed anthracnose, so I had additional leaf fall to contend with in the spring. What a pain. If I had known ten years ago what I know now, that darn tree would be compost by this time. So do a little extra research before you commit to any plant big enough to kill you when it falls.

Shrubs, Vines, and the Rest

Begin the selection of the major shrubs in your landscape by determining what functions they are to fulfill. Most often, we use large shrubs to hide something we don't want to see. While mature trees can screen items from their lowest branches to the top of their canopy, there aren't too many eyesores with such convenient dimensions. Shrubs, on the other hand, branch from the ground up, and many can get quite tall, fifteen feet or more. But don't use a twenty-foot shrub when all you want is an eight-foot hedge. There are plenty of plants that top out at eight feet, or five feet, or even two, if that's what is called for.

Vines can fulfill many of the same purposes as the taller shrubs, and they are a small garden designer's best friends. They cover and soften a fence or wall without taking up space that you may want for other plants. Whereas most shrubs are

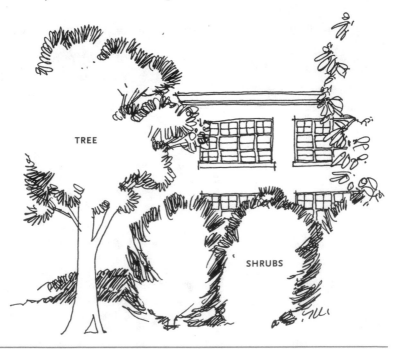

TREE

SHRUBS

**Use both trees and shrubs to screen ground-to-sky uglies
like this prison cellblock.**

roughly as wide as they are tall, there are vines that can grow to twenty feet and only get a couple of feet wide.

In selecting shrubs and vines, don't forget to take longevity into account. If you use only a few short-lived plants, it will be no big deal to replace them in a few years. But if they are the backbone of your scheme, there'll be quite a hole when they are gone, and replanting will be a chore.

Begin by drawing in and then identifying the larger shrubs and vines, then work your way toward the smaller ones.

A word here about evergreen versus deciduous plants: I usually start by determining the location for, and then specifying the species of, evergreen plants first (not just trees, but shrubs and groundcovers too). These will be the structural "bones" of your planting design, so use them to screen the ugliest of uglies, soften the harshest architecture, and create strategic interest in the winter months. But don't make the common beginner's mistake of thinking that all plants must hold onto their leaves year-round or they aren't pulling their weight. The best plants for fall color and spring bloom are all deciduous, and in my opinion the changing nature of a garden throughout the seasons is what distinguishes it from other art forms or aesthetic experiences. If we could design a garden that looked exactly the same every day, why would we ever go out there? There would be nothing new to see.

QUICK TIP

In drawing your plan, don't sketch in each one-gallon or four-inch potted plant. First, you will have such a wealth of visual information in the resulting drawing that you'll never be able to make sense of it. Second, after your larger plants are in, you'll find that the area designated for the smaller ones has moved, shrunk, or expanded. And third, it is much easier to design your smaller plants "on the ground." You *will* need to know how many of the smaller plants to purchase, though, and you can determine this by figuring the square footage each will occupy at maturity and then dividing the total square footage to be planted by that number. Where there will be several different types of small-scale plants to be planted in masses, just estimate the percentage of the total square footage each will occupy.

The selection of the small shrubs, groundcovers, and perennials is less critical than that of the larger shrubs and trees—the failure of a small plant leaves only a small hole in the landscape, so you can experiment more with these fellows. Just avoid invasive scourges such as ivy, *Vinca major*, polygonum *(Persicaria capitata)*, and the like.

Selecting Winning Plant Combinations

First, try not to get overly fixated on flowers for color and interest. Different plant forms and textures, colored foliage, and interesting bark or branching patterns are greatly underutilized elements. Drama and intrigue can spring from the juxtaposition of a wispy, delicate feather grass *(Stipa tenuissima)* with the impossibly shiny mirror plant *(Coprosma repens)*, or the contrast of the chartreuse *Spiraea* 'Limemound' with the burgundy of a purple smoke tree, *Cotinus coggygria purpurea*.

Try to avoid seizing upon one inspiration to the exclusion of all others. An all-grasses garden, for example, is greatly livened up by the inclusion of plants that are completely different in every way (my favorite is *Sedum spectabile*, a fleshy succulent that nonetheless looks right at home amid its wispy friends).

Probably the worst design sin you can commit is to try to include one sample of every plant you love. Remember my dictum "Be disciplined"? This is really the time to exercise that restraint. Most smaller plants should be planted in multiples, rather than singly (and the smaller the plant, the more you'll need). This is because while a single tree is large enough to command presence and dominate space, a single shrub can rarely do that.

There are exceptions, of course. One Cécile Brunner rose is just plenty for almost anyone, and a single snowball viburnum *(Viburnum opulus* 'Roseum') can draw attention to itself just fine, thank you. But a lone agapanthus is barely noticeable, while seven or eight will make you want to get out the camera. A good rule of thumb is to mass at least three of any one kind of plant.

And the larger the yard, the larger the size of the plant to which this rule applies. After all, in a really vast estate, even one Cécile Brunner would look lost and forlorn.

The importance of massing is even more critical with small plants than with large ones. Whereas three specimens of *Rosa mutabilis* will catch the eye, it may take seven or eight plants of Santa Barbara daisy *(Erigeron karvinskianus)* to make any kind of an impact in the landscape. Luckily, small plants are usually closer to the viewer or garden stroller, or the numbers needed would be even higher.

Speaking of that, of course you already figured out that tall plants go behind short ones, didn't you? Plantings should ascend gradually from lowest to tallest as they get farther from the path, lawn, or any other viewing area. Of course, you can always punctuate with an occasional high-branching tree, but

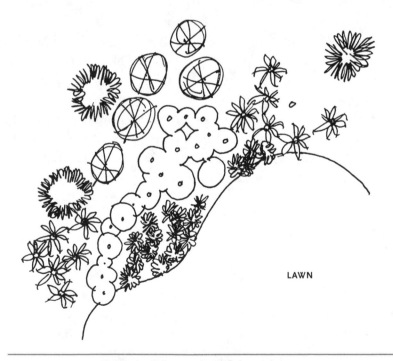

LAWN

"Massing" in groups of three or more

Plant in ascending order of height.

don't make the mistake of having all your precious six-inch-high crocuses obscured by the robust hellebores you planted in front of them.

In addition to massing your plantings, repeat some of your plant choices throughout the yard. This is a particularly useful trick to tie in one side of the driveway with the other, or to connect disparate parts of a large garden. A repeating element such as a cluster of fieldstone boulders and "Silver Lace" society garlic *(Tulbaghia violacea)*, for example, can be placed at the beginnings and ends of paths, at the base of steps and arbors, and in the curve of a walkway. In this way, important points are emphasized as they are linked.

In general, it's good to use odd-numbered groupings of plants. The eye of the garden viewer is apt to try to separate and compare the individuals in even-numbered groupings (up to a point; after about six items, the eye can no longer play this trick). This tendency to divide even-numbered groupings can be played to your advantage as a way of drawing attention to an object, however. For example, putting a topiary on each side of an entrance will emphasize the doorway in between. Symmetry, even in a primarily asymmetrical yard, is a powerful tool for focusing attention on a particular spot.

You should group plants with similar water needs together in what are called "hydrazones" so that they can be watered as one group. For example, you wouldn't want to put a drought-loving plant like *Fremontodendron*, which can rot from a single emitter, on the same irrigation station as a fuchsia, whose thirst is legendary. The geographical division of your yard into different irrigation stations should correspond to the physical separation of your plants by water needs. (We'll cover this topic in more detail in the section "What Plants Want" in Chapter 6, Irrigation Systems.)

I could go on and on with tricks and tips for choosing and placing plants, but in the end it is best for you to take your own chances, learn from your mistakes, and become the gardener you are meant to be. You'll develop your own outlook and expertise, and become the king, or queen, of your own green fiefdom. A garden is a dynamic, unpredictable, and interdependent creature.

The goal of your planting plan is to establish a framework for the inevitable fine-tuning you'll do as the garden matures, as your tastes change, and as you get to know all the quirks of your own unique plot of land. So don't obsess too much over choosing exactly the right plant for each spot. And expect that some plants are going to die. (Just a few, a few. It's to be expected.)

You don't have to become a horticultural authority to make good plant choices. Talk to knowledgeable nursery people, observe what does well in your area, consult the *Sunset Western Garden Book* religiously, and expect to continue to learn as the plants grow (or don't).

IN CONCLUSION

Whether your final landscape plan takes the form of one sheet of paper jammed chock full of information or a series of loose sketches, you are now "done" with the paper part of your landscape design. Of course, as the installation progresses you may find it necessary to refine your plan at the drawing board once or even twice more, but for now you've gone as far as you can go before breaking ground.

However, before you don your sunbonnet and begin wielding heavy implements, let's take a moment to talk about planning the installation of the project you've so carefully designed.

 Chapter 3

Phasing the Construction

When to Do What

There is no way to do justice to the many trades involved in even the simplest of backyard construction projects. Luckily for you, however, well-written books abound on every topic imaginable, from waterfalls to wind chimes and from gazebos to garden gates. Buy them. What I can do is help you coordinate the timing and integration of such projects into the greater landscape, and help you avoid some of the more preventable mistakes that seem to get handed down from one generation to the next.

At what point in the process of landscaping your yard should you build your deck? Pour a patio? Make a pond? In general, these endeavors are best undertaken after your demolition and rough grading is done, and before you tackle irrigation and soil preparation. In some cases, however, a construction project can disrupt or alter your grading so completely that it's best to get the building done before you do any serious soil moving at all.

I'll begin with the project types that should be done earliest in the scheme of things and end with those that can be done last or even as afterthoughts.

SITE PREPARATION

Removing all the unwanted clutter in your yard is the first step toward fulfilling your garden dream. The goal is to make your yard as blank as the base plan you started out with.

Removing Plantings

One of the first questions to ask yourself is whether you will use herbicides in your attempt to purge your yard of unwanted squatters. This will depend both on your personal convictions and on the particular pest you harbor. I've seen ardent environmentalists dispense with their principles (and swear me to secrecy) when the dollars they would spend upholding their convictions stopped making sense. But if the plants you'll be removing are docile and cooperative, there may be no need to resort to poisoning them.

QUICK TIP
If ivy is your curse, be aware that the waxiness of the leaves renders them impermeable to the absorption of most sprays, so you must first provide a point of entry by mowing or otherwise cutting into the stand. Spray quickly, before the wounds have time to heal over.

Some plants we love—Mexican evening primrose, Japanese anemone (*Anemone hybrida*), and periwinkle, to name a few—can be as hard to eradicate as those we all know to hate—Bermuda grass, blackberries, and anise (*Pimpinella anisum*). Remember, a weed is just any plant in the wrong place. With any such weedy plant, it will be important to kill and/or remove the entire plant, since any parts left in the soil will generate a new infestation. You can spray such plants with a systemic herbicide before physical removal, but even then chances are they will still return to make your life miserable. If you'd prefer not to use herbicides, it's even more important to leave *no* body parts of your enemy on the battlefield (and be prepared to be at war for years to come).

Try to remove your leafy foes six months to a year before you begin installing your landscaping. This will allow you to track down every bit of the enemy before it is surrounded by the desirable new plants you want to protect. A crafty technique is to physically remove the plant pest and then invite it back—by watering, or perhaps even fertilizing—so that you can attack the stragglers anew. If you can do this several times, you greatly increase the likelihood of true eradication. If you do this and then mound soil over the area of infestation, your chances of success are further increased. Covering your enemy with dirt makes it difficult for the already weakened remaining shoots to reach the sun and photosynthesize, thereby replenishing their depleted energy stores. Plus, then you won't have to·contend with their roots as you grade, trench, and plant.

If there are extensive plantings or undergrowth to remove, you may want to use power equipment such as chainsaws, high-weed mowers, or even a tractor (to pull out or push over full-grown small trees and shrubs).

In most cases, it is far more trouble to grub out the stump of large shrubs than it's worth. It doesn't solve the real problem of pervasive roots throughout the soil profile, and it can take hours and hours of time better spent in more rewarding, productive pursuits. Instead, simply cut plants down to the ground, as low as you can. With many plants, that will be the kiss of death. Others will rise up again and must then either be sprayed with a systemic herbicide or repeatedly hacked back until they give up hope. If there is a compelling reason to get the stumps out, it may be possible to unearth an entire

> **QUICK TIP**
>
> Don't make the mistake of removing all the top growth of an unwanted plant and *then* trying to get the stump out. You need the top of the plant to use as a handle. Instead, trim back as needed for a good grip, then dig in a circle all around the plant. Once this is done, have one person attempt to pull the plant over while the other furiously hacks away at the roots at the base of the root ball on the opposing side. Works great.

plant by wrapping a stout chain around it and driving off. But do not do this with your little Toyota—unless you want a new one. I blew out the rear end of my old Ford 150 pulling out oceans of junipers (the vermin of the plant world) in the '80s. Okay, maybe it was worth it . . .

Saving Plants

There will be some plants that are so desirable or unique that you will want to save them. Or perhaps nearly all your plants are worth keeping, but you still want to re-landscape. The problem is, every plant in the ground is a plant that is in the way. What to do? The answer is to dig them up, lay them down, and "heel them in" (cover their roots with newspaper, compost, or soil). Get as much of the root ball of each plant as you can, and cut back the top to compensate for the loss of those roots you left behind. If you are saving perennials, cut them back hard.

Keep your stockpile moist. Once you've completed your soil preparation, grading, trenching, and so on and are finally ready to plant, sort through and see which, if any, plants you still want to use. If you forgot to water them, see "Hauling" below. But if they are alive, even if they look terrible, they'll probably make it. Cut into the wood—if it is green under the bark, they'll probably come round. And most perennials will be just fine (except lavenders). As a rule of thumb, the more deep-rooted or drought-tolerant a plant is, the less thrilled it will be with your efforts to save it.

Clearing Construction Debris

You should probably rent a demolition hammer (jackhammer) to break paving up into manageable chunks. Sledgehammers are fine for small areas, but using one is more dangerous and tiring than using power equipment. Concrete and masonry are expensive to haul, and some dumps won't take them at all, so you should try to find a home for them in your yard, if at all possible. (If rebar was used, this won't be feasible.) Old concrete pieces make an attractive dry-stacked wall, or can be used as stepping-stones in paths or sitting areas. Bricks, rocks, and rubble can be used as "clean fill" or to line a drainage channel. It will pay to get creative.

Rock mulches are another material you should try to recycle

within the confines of your own property, since they, too, are heavy to load and haul. If you are cursed with an especially ugly material—perhaps that sparkly white rock so favored in the '70s?—you can use it as the base for a path, covering it with something more attractive, such as crushed rock or decomposed granite. If there is no way to reuse old rock, you can try giving it away, or, if there isn't too much, you can spread it about and till it in.

Demolition of wooden structures like decks will go much more quickly with a few tools like a crowbar and a heavy iron digging bar for leverage. Do be careful.

Hauling

If all your debris is the compostable sort, it may work to rent a chipper and make your own mulch if there is an out-of-the-way place to hold it till it can be used. Or, if you live in the country, you can pile up your brush in the back forty and declare it bird habitat (birds love mounds of brush). Some counties will still even allow you to burn your yard waste; but do so only in the glare of my disapproval, and call the county to confirm before you torch that pile.

If you rent a dumpster, be aware that they won't let you fill it with really heavy stuff like dirt or concrete. Dumpsters are a good option if you need to toss stuff over a long period of time, such as over the course of a remodeling project. But most people will want to get everything out at once and so would be better served by hauling debris off.

If you have your own truck, you will find it worth your while to load it carefully in order to minimize the number of trips you'll make to your local landfill. Break down or chop stuff so it'll take up less space, and load material so that it is all aligned in the same direction. A single intact tree limb, or a couple of crossed timbers, can fill the whole bed of most trucks. Save really bulky, awkward items to go on top of your load, where it won't matter how much space they'll take up.

Separate your recyclables as you load to save time at the dump. Call the landfill or transfer station ahead of time to see what categories they do or do not accept. In some locales, your dump fee will be waived if yours is a clean, compostable load. Cover the whole mess with a tarp, or even an old sheet, especially if there is loose garbage that could blow out. Letting trash fly off the back of a truck is considered littering, and is fined as such.

Oh, and tie everything down. I'll never forget crossing a bridge and glancing in my rearview mirror to see an entire *tree* fall off my truck. Or the time a car pulled alongside me on the freeway, the driver honking and gesturing. When I pulled over I discovered my wheelbarrow hanging over the sideboards by its *wheel*. Or even the time (in the days when dogs ran free) when we heard a scrabbling on the roof of the cab like Santa's little reindeer. And realized that our Dingding was *on top of the cab*. Yes, it's good to tie down everything, trash and precious animal companions alike.

POOLS AND PONDS

A swimming pool should go in before you do anything—and I mean *anything*—else to your yard. The destruction caused by the heavy equipment can be total; and furthermore, you may need to find a home for at least part of the excavated dirt, which will alter any grading plans you might have made.

You will be amazed at the mountain of soil the excavation of even a small pond can create. If you are planning a waterfall and your ground is flat, you will need all this dirt to create a slope for the beginning of the fall. But if you just want a flat reflective surface, then you will need to find a home for the soil you've displaced. Hauling dirt is an expensive option of last resort. For this reason, I normally dig the pond before doing major grading work. On the other hand, it's critical to know exactly where your final grade will be because it will affect the finished water level of the pond. So you may want to dig the rough shape of the pond early on, and then fine-tune the digging and finish the installation after grading is complete.

Professional pond installers debate fiercely over the comparative merits of liners and concrete. Concrete aficionados extol the longevity of their medium as well as its more natural appearance. Liner lovers swear by their product's ease of installation and lack of leaks. Myself, I like liners. I've noticed that all concrete ponds leak sooner or later, and when they do, the leaks are almost impossible to find and fix. And because concrete ponds are just plain harder to build, I think most people are better off with user-friendly, homeowner-forgiving liners. Just buy the best quality stuff you can afford. I do understand the aesthetic objections to liner ponds, however. Seeing exposed plastic along a pond is about as attractive as finding candy wrappers in Yosemite.

The trick to hiding a pond liner is all in the digging of the shelf that holds the boulders that hide the liner. Got that? Make the shelf big, so it can accommodate big boulders if you need them. Make it level to itself so that none of the boulders are either completely submerged or overexposed when the pond is filled (water makes the ultimate contour line). And then make sure that the top lip of the pond is exactly level to *itself*, too, so

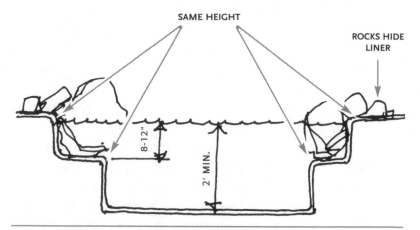

"Correct" pond liner installation

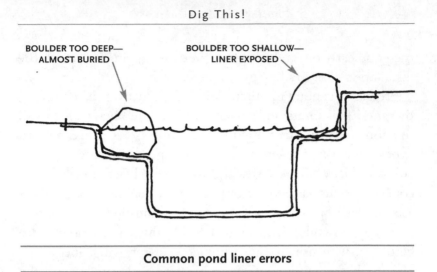

BOULDER TOO DEEP—
ALMOST BURIED

BOULDER TOO SHALLOW—
LINER EXPOSED

Common pond liner errors

that you don't have to fill in or dig out the grade underneath the liner once you've filled the pond with water.

One more trick I've learned several times the hard way: Never, ever trim your liner until the pond is full and all your rocks are in. The weight of the water and rocks tends to pull liner material into the pond, and if you've trimmed it too close you could end up with the edge of the liner below water level, with the result that the pond will lose water until it reaches the level of the liner.

RETAINING WALLS

The purpose of constructing retaining walls is to alter the lay of the land, and so naturally they should be built before you embark on any other serious grading work. They absolutely cannot be added later without disrupting the entire landscape. You should have some idea of the final grading scheme for your lot—including the walls—before you begin. But since their construction will itself displace so much earth, resulting in either an excess or a dearth of material, save your pick-and-shovel grading work till the walls are in. You'll find that even the best-laid grading plan may need major tweaking afterwards.

The single most important thing to know about retaining walls is that they are only as long-lived as their drainage is sound. That is, you can build a wall using eight-by-eight posts spaced two feet apart, sunk in concrete three feet down, but if you neglect to provide a passage for water to escape from behind that fortress, it will tilt and topple in no time at all. I had a client who built and then backfilled an (illegal) ten-foot-high wall in his back yard so he could play a little croquet of an evening. The project demanded the importation of vast quantities of fill and the rental of earthmovers and compacters, to say nothing of an entire summer's leisure time. But did my hardworking hero install drainage behind his Great Wall? No, he did not; and when I saw it again after a single rainy season it was already leaning more than that tower over in Pisa.

Wooden Walls

Wooden retaining walls are usually the fastest and least expensive to build. Create a French drain (see "French Drains" in Chapter 4, Grading and Drainage) behind the wall that will be channeled into your yard's drainage system. Make sure you backfill with gravel up the entire back of the wall so that all soil that would be in contact with wood is met with porous rock instead.

Do not skimp on timber size, spacing, or concrete for your posts. It is the posts that do the true work of holding up the wall.

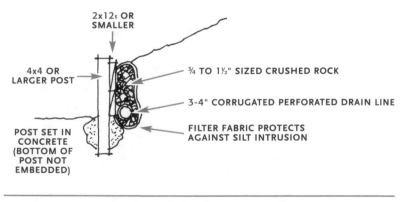

2x12s OR SMALLER

4x4 OR LARGER POST

POST SET IN CONCRETE (BOTTOM OF POST NOT EMBEDDED)

¾ TO 1½" SIZED CRUSHED ROCK

3-4" CORRUGATED PERFORATED DRAIN LINE

FILTER FABRIC PROTECTS AGAINST SILT INTRUSION

Drainage behind retaining wall

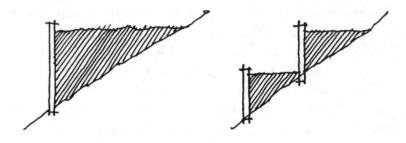

One tall versus two short retaining walls on the same slope

Do not attempt to build a wall more than three feet high. Walls higher than three feet require permits and are more difficult to engineer. Either hire a professional, or retain the slope with a series of lower terraces.

Stone Walls

Stone walls can be either dry-stacked or mortared. The weight of the stones gives dry-stacked walls their strength and stability. Use the largest stones on the bottom course, set six inches or so into the earth, and slant the wall back into the slope a couple of inches for every foot of height to ensure that gravity doesn't take its toll prematurely. Backfill as you go. A dry-stacked wall does not require a drain because water can escape from between the rocks.

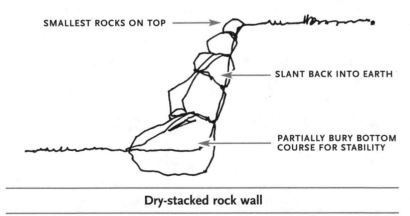

SMALLEST ROCKS ON TOP

SLANT BACK INTO EARTH

PARTIALLY BURY BOTTOM COURSE FOR STABILITY

Dry-stacked rock wall

Mortared walls will need a sturdy concrete foundation. With mortared stone walls, it is a good idea to create "weep holes" for the water to escape, though I'd also provide a French drain behind the wall to be on the safe side.

STEPS

The construction of steps can barely disturb the landscape at all, or it can displace large amounts of soil that must be disposed of. The nature of the slope to be stepped and the layout of the treads and risers will dictate how much disruption results, and thus the timing of the installation. We usually build steps early on just so we can use them as we go about landscaping the rest of the site.

> **QUICK TIP**
> The tread plus twice the riser should equal twenty-six inches.

Occasionally, and indeed miraculously, your ideal tread-to-riser ratio will just exactly match the angle of the slope you are working on. But don't count on it.

If you want low, broad steps up a steep slope, you will end up building huge header walls to hold back the slope on the sides (and you will have lots of dirt to find a home for). If you want crisp, no-nonsense, gotta-go–type steps up a gentle rise, be prepared to cool your heels on a few landings so that the lay of the land can catch up to your impatient ascension.

> **ANOTHER QUICK TIP**
> Always begin your steps at the bottom of the slope. That way, if your pencil wasn't quite as sharp as it should have been, you can fudge with landings, rather than trying to build on air.

It will be easier to build your steps if you can hit on a tread-to-riser ratio that can accomplish all the rise (vertical distance) you need in something close to the amount of tread (horizontal distance) you have available. So sharpen that pencil. Be aware that for residential work, risers more than eight inches high or treads less than nine inches deep just won't work. (In fact, you'll be happiest with six-inch risers, if that's at all possible.)

GARDEN STRUCTURES

Buildings such as toolsheds and playhouses, gazebos and tea-houses should generally be built fairly early on—after major grading and before the sitting or paving areas that are often placed in conjunction with them. Take the time to site such structures with care, since there is almost nothing (with the possible exception of swimming pools) that will make such a visual impact in the finished landscape. And buildings, like big trees and pools, are not easily or cheaply moved.

In general, any buildings in the garden should be sympathetic in character and color palette to the biggest building of them all—your house. If your house is essentially a big undifferentiated stucco box, a frilly, ornate Victorian gazebo just isn't going to cut it. Better to choose something with clean, simple lines—a Japanese teahouse, perhaps. You don't have to copy the style of your house, but don't make a mockery of it, either. The building(s) you choose will set the tone for the whole garden.

A good place to get ideas and even plans for garden structures is in the back of gardening magazines such as *Fine Gardening*, *Sunset*, and *Horticulture*. You'd be amazed at the diversity of designs and the quality of workmanship. I've had several clients who went this route and were delighted by both the process (especially by having so many plans to choose from) and the outcome (unusual and distinctive buildings).

PAVED SITTING AREAS

Paved areas affect grading and drainage in three ways. Their construction frequently disrupts the existing flow of water on the site (they're often located directly in a drainage swale). Then there can be large amounts of excavated soil to import or export, depending on the depth of base material and the final grade of the paved area itself. Finally, their impervious surfaces increase the amount of runoff you will have to provide for.

Paving should be installed early on in the course of your landscaping, with extra attention paid to any possible future needs. (Paved areas can block access for future underground utilities such as water and electricity.) Paving is so permanent, immovable, and landscape-altering that you should think long and hard about its placement and function before committing yourself to its construction.

Concrete work is not for the faint of heart or the first-timer. There is just too much that can go wrong, too quickly and too irrevocably, for it to be a good do-it-yourself project. If you must do your own concrete work, stick to the prep work and form building, and get help with the pour. But most people will be happier restricting their efforts to paver stones or brick-on-sand applications, where mistakes are more forgiving and the pace is more leisurely.

Four things to remember about concrete paving:

• All paving is only as strong as its base is solid.
• You can never install too many sleeves, or too large a sleeve. (A sleeve, or "chase," as it is sometimes called, is a pipe laid under paving through which other pipes can be inserted.) Sleeves should be at least two inches in diameter, and three inches is usually better. How many times have I had to tunnel under walkways, or cut through driveways, for the lack of a sleeve?

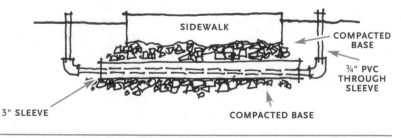

Using a sleeve (chase) under a sidewalk

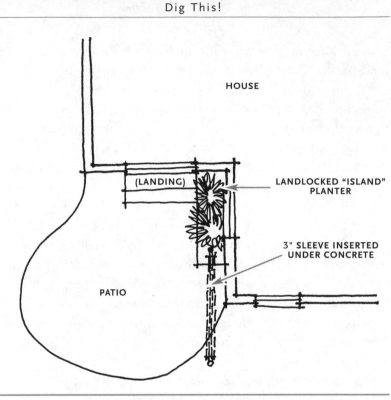

Top view of sleeve (chase) under patio

- If the final grade of a paved surface is too high (because you didn't want to remove soil to accommodate the base rock), you will have to adjust the grade that surrounds it accordingly. If this means importing huge amounts of topsoil, you may be better off making the grade of the patio lower—and excavating more for the base—than trucking in all that fill.
- Finally, don't forget to accommodate the drainage water displaced when paving interrupts the flow of surface water. It's often easier to run a former swale underneath a new patio in the form of a four- or six-inch pipe than to reroute it around the paving.

DECKS

Decks are so much more forgiving than paving. Because water flows through them and because they impact the ground plane only at their supporting piers, they alter existing drainage patterns very little. The main problem I find with decks is that people build them before they grade. And once the decks are built, it's oh-so-hard to correct even a simple drainage problem, crawling around on your tummy under there with the all the cobwebs, bumping your head on exposed nails while trying not to think about black widows. So do your drainage work *before* you build the deck.

The nice thing about decks is that you always have room to slip a little pipe underneath them, so you don't need to sweat too hard anticipating every water line and electrical conduit needed before you begin construction.

Use countersunk screws to attach the decking itself. That way, you can easily remove boards as needed. What's more important, you avoid one of the great hazards to barefoot users: the popped-up nailhead. The other great foe of the shoeless is splinters. Look into using Trex, a recycled lumber/plastic product I wish I'd bought stock in. It lasts forever, needs no maintenance, and is splinter free.

PATHS

Paved paths should be installed at the same time as paved sitting areas, since it is so much more efficient to do one pour than two. But the timing for other kinds of paths will vary. Because paths often define the spaces in a landscape, they are the first things I lay out after grading. Then sometimes I go ahead and install the irrigation and do my soil preparation before I do the walks, and sometimes I put the walks in first.

The simplest walkways are just a passage through the plantings, surfaced in the same mulch that is used around the plants. Such walks should still be graded so they will be amenable to foot traffic, even if no other work is called for (see illustration on next page).

Next simplest are paths made of aggregate materials such as crushed rock or decomposed granite. These walks usually

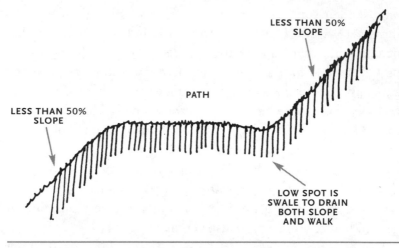

LESS THAN 50%
SLOPE

PATH

LESS THAN 50%
SLOPE

LOW SPOT IS
SWALE TO DRAIN
BOTH SLOPE
AND WALK

Grading for path on slope

require a bit more grading, both along their length and from side to side, to eliminate steep slopes so that the materials stay put. I usually do the grading for both the landscape and the paths at the same time, and then install borders of head-sized field-stone or bender board to delineate such walkways. Then I proceed with the rest of the landscaping and wait to fill the paths with material until the very end. That way, dirt and mulch don't get mixed in with the rock or decomposed granite.

QUICK TIP

Add a little binder, such as cement, to your decomposed granite to keep it in place.

When I make stepping-stone walkways, I lay out and grade them as needed and then wait until most of the wheelbarrow traffic is over before I place the stones. That way I reduce the

CRUSHED ROCK

MULCH

EXISTING GRADE

OPTIONAL AVIARY WIRE

"HEADSIZE" FIELDSTONE ROCK

Crushed rock path with fieldstone border

chances of a prize piece of flagstone getting cracked by an over-loaded wheelbarrow, and the stones stay cleaner.

In gopher country, any path made of composite materials should be underlaid with aviary wire or hardware cloth to prevent mounds from spoiling the grade.

DRY CREEK BEDS

The timing for installing a dry creek bed will be twofold. Dig the channel when you are doing your primary grading, since a dry creek bed looks plausible (and makes sense) only if it is in fact a waterway in the rainy season. Give some thought to how a real dry creek bed looks. Make it meander a bit; create some spots where your imaginary water might eddy about.

Wait until all your dirt work is done before installing the rock, so you don't unnecessarily impede access across the yard. I usually put big boulders in the creek bed at the same time that I place other rocks in the yard. (And do use boulders elsewhere in the landscape—it looks unnatural to have one area full of rocks without an outcropping or two elsewhere.)

Meandering dry creek bed with boulders, river cobbles, and gravel (mixed sizes)

I hold off on bringing in the cobbles and smaller stones until I'm pretty sure we're done making a mess of things. This is usually about the same time we'd be mulching—that is, after planting and the final grading. If you do it any sooner, you run the risk of getting clods of dirt down in the streambed and creating a nice home for weeds.

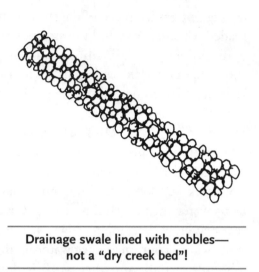

Drainage swale lined with cobbles— not a "dry creek bed"!

In fact, the only time I ever consistently use weed fabric is underneath the cobbles in a dry creek bed, where the risk of weeds is great and the weight of the rocks will ensure that the fabric stays put. (See "Mulch: The Gift That Keeps on Giving" in Chapter 7 for my thoughts—mostly negative—regarding other uses of weed fabric.)

One last tip on dry creek beds. A good one can be a dynamic focal point and solicit oohs and ahs from the neighbors. A bad one can look silly, as in "Hasn't he ever been to the mountains?" So study up a bit on real creek beds, and stay loose when placing those rocks.

FENCES

Fences can be installed at any time. But often it's nice to hold off on fencing till the very end of your landscaping project so that your access remains as open as possible. It can save a lot of time and wheelbarrow trips to get materials delivered right to where they're needed. Sometimes I even remove sections of existing fence when the access would otherwise present an insurmountable obstacle.

No matter when you install your fence, be sure you have a couple of inches of clearance between the soil or mulch and any nontreated wood (typically the fence boards themselves). And make sure your posts are set deeply and well. Of particular importance is the concrete at the post. It should not encase the bottom of the post, and should be sloped away from the post where it meets the ground. This simple precaution will greatly increase the longevity of your posts and thus your fence.

Of course, before you dig a single hole you should have a friendly chat with your neighbors and verify the location of your property lines. And be aware that many communities have ordinances that ban fences over six feet high for side and back yards. In addition, many prohibit fences entirely in front yards.

LOW-VOLTAGE LIGHTING

Magazines geared to landscape contractors abound with articles with titles like "Lighting Boosts the Bottom Line" and "Low Voltage, High Profit," which tout the profitability of low-voltage landscape lighting. I always feel sorry for the home-owner whose fiscal pain is meant to fuel my gain. As offensive as such articles may be, however, their existence should clue you, the crafty do-it-yourselfer, to an Opportunity. Don't be fooled by the outrageous prices charged by (a few) greedy contractors; low-voltage lighting is child's play to install.

Low-voltage lighting systems are so noninvasive that they can easily be installed well after your landscape is complete. In fact, I would recommend against installing lighting too early on. Because most of your lighting cable will be "direct burial" (that is, buried just under the soil surface), it can easily get cut or nicked if you put it in while there's still digging or soil work to do.

We install lighting systems just prior to mulching, after the final grade has been done. Run your wire in easy-to-remember and unlikely-to-be-disturbed locations: along walkways, against the house, next to the border for the lawn. If you must cross a large "unprotected" expanse, it's best to put the wire in a conduit. We sometimes run it like the wire for the irrigation timer, taping it to the underside of the irrigation mainline pipe, where it will be protected.

The two biggest mistakes people make with outdoor lighting are buying cheap fixtures and underdesigning the capacity of their systems.

The solution to the first problem is easy: Don't purchase those cheap kits at the big-box stores. The fittings are junk, and in any case, why should you limit yourself to what comes in the box? Buy from the same sources the professionals use—usually an irrigation store—and custom-design your system to fit your actual wants and needs. The cost of a single fixture may well be what you'd pay for the whole package at Cheap Is Us, but you'll still have a functioning system by next Christmastime. And the one after that, too.

The solution to the second problem isn't really all that hard, either. Electricity behaves a lot like water. The sizes of your cable and transformer are analogous to the sizes of your

QUICK TIP

With lighting, less is more. For walkways, you only need to see where the path leads, not every pebble of its composition. Elsewhere, remember that one or two spotlights create drama and magic; more than that, and you merely have illumination. When all is revealed, much is lost.

pipes and valves in an irrigation system. With irrigation, if you want to run a lot of heads at once, you need big pipes, a big valve, and lots of gallons per minute. To run a lot of lights at once, you need thick cable and a beefy transformer. In both cases, the longer your runs, the larger your components need to be. If you buy your supplies at a real store, they'll have the charts you need to calculate the number of amps and watts and volts you should plan for. And just remember: Overdesign (as I'll urge you to do with your irrigation in Chapter 6), so you'll have the flexibility to add to your system later should you so desire.

RAISED BEDS

Raised beds can be built as soon as the preliminary grading is complete. The best dimensions, both for ease of construction and ease of use, seem to be four feet wide by eight feet long and a foot deep. Line the bottom with aviary wire or hardware cloth in gopher country, and fill with a top-quality soil mix.

When a vegetable or cut-flower garden is to be made up of raised beds, I'll supply it with its own irrigation line. I adapt a drip system to use soaker hoses, which I coil on the soil surface with an individual shutoff for each bed.

BOULDERS

Boulders should be installed sometime after rough grading and soil preparation and before planting. Sometimes I'll put them in before irrigation, designing the sprinkler-head layout around them, and other times I'll put them in afterward, being sure not to block a head with a large rock.

The largest fieldstone boulder that is movable by two people, some steel digging bars, and lots of grunting will be about twenty by thirty inches. If you want larger rocks (and rocks can be too small, but rarely too large), arrange for equipment. Most landscape supply places that sell rock will supply a forklift at delivery for another hundred bucks or so, and will place each rock as you specify (within reason). You should have the spots

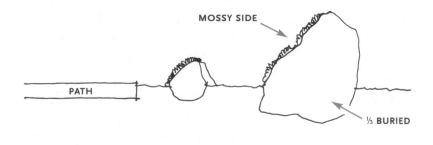

Side view of typical boulder placement

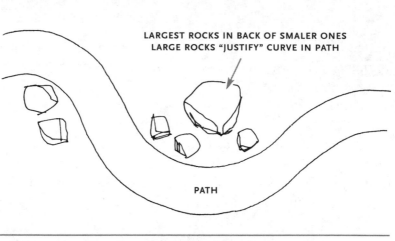

LARGEST ROCKS IN BACK OF SMALER ONES
LARGE ROCKS "JUSTIFY" CURVE IN PATH

PATH

Top view of typical boulder placement

for the boulders already dug out before they arrive, to save tempers (theirs) and time (which is your money).

"Plant" your boulders so that the bottom quarter or so is buried. (Later, after you've mulched, about a third will be below ground.) Cluster boulders in groups of three to seven, with the larger ones toward the back (a small rock can easily be lost among plantings as they grow). And be sure to turn each boulder so that its best side faces forward. I also like to use low, flat boulders as impromptu sitting spots at the edges of paths.

ARBORS, TRELLISES, AND BENCHES

These elements are relatively nondisruptive to the landscape, so they can be installed pretty much any time. Of course, if you want to plant a vine in conjunction with such a structure, it's best to build it before you plant. And you wouldn't want to install anything before major grading, for the usual obvious reasons.

The timing of any construction project in the overall landscape scheme will sometimes be determined by factors outside your control, particularly if you are contracting out some portions of the work. So don't sweat it if the irrigation goes in before your walks are done (you can always adjust the paths to the heads, instead of vice versa) or if your boulders are delivered before you've finished your drainage work.

Landscaping is an inexact science at best, so remaining flexible is a valuable talent to develop. If you can just avoid the two biggies—building a deck on top of a drainage problem, and pouring a patio without sleeves—I won't have written this chapter in vain.

 Chapter 4

Grading and Drainage

Giving the Water a Place to Go

I t seems ironic in a region as parched as Northern California that we should have to worry about excess water. But even desert landscapes get rain, and when they do, every dry wash can become the locus of a flash flood. Perhaps we don't need to fret about flash floods here. But we do get rain, and because most of our precipitation occurs over a two- or three-month period, during that time it could practically be the tropics around here. The reason California turns brown—oops, I mean gold—in the summer is not that we don't get enough rain. We get plenty of rain, as much as many places that are still green in July. The difference is, we don't get rain in *July*.

Grading and drainage are probably the most poorly understood components of a landscape installation project. I am always amazed at how many people throw plants in the ground, or build a deck, without checking and correcting the lay of the land first. (At least plants can be moved or worked around, but once a deck is built, it is almost impossible to correct the grade beneath it.) It's easy to overlook the whole subject of drainage. To the unpracticed eye, a garden that collects water looks just fine. However, landscapes in which drainage has not been addressed suffer from high plant mortality as well as unnecessary sogginess. And houses themselves are subject to an even more insidious host of ills, the most fearsome of which is water under the house, the source of problems ranging from mildew to settling foundations.

Grading is a continuous process. Over the course of your landscaping project, you will grade not once but many times. Indeed, it sometimes seems as if all we do is move soil from one spot to another, and then in some instances back again.

Ideally, you will do a rough grading after any necessary demolition is done and before you prepare your soil, so that you don't have two inches of good soil in one area and three feet in another. You will rough-grade again before you install your irrigation, so that the pipe you installed eighteen inches deep doesn't end up at six. You will grade scrupulously and religiously before planting, so that an aquaphobic plant like fremontodendron doesn't end up in a low spot, and because once the plants are in, the grade around them absolutely cannot be changed. You will grade and level right before you sod or seed your lawn. And, lastly, you will grade before you mulch, so that when the material is spread it out flat it isn't an inch thick in some spots and a foot thick in others.

TERMS OF ENDEARMENT

Grading

The term "grading" refers to the process of moving soil, usually to improve the flow of water. It is the main means by which we attain proper drainage. It can be as simple as shoveling off high spots and raking in low ones, or as complex as creating a system of slopes (to enhance runoff) and swales (to carry the runoff away).

Often, grading is used as an aesthetic device. Pleasing contours and topographical changes can delight the eye and create interest in formerly flat sites. Creating a series of low terraces down a gentle slope, or a group of gentle berms along a path, may increase both the utility and the beauty of your garden. There are even artists who do "earthworks"—sculptures in which the earth itself is molded, as one would shape clay.

Grading can also be a science. Determining the correct amount of fill needed behind a retaining wall, or how many steps are needed down a steep slope, requires the use of formulas and calculations quite capable of boggling most minds. The "Grading and Drainage" section of the landscape architect's licensing exam is the most dreaded, the most often failed and retaken, of them all.

Drainage

The term "drainage" refers to the ability of your landscape to shed excess water from irrigation and rainfall. Any yard in which there is still standing water more than a few hours after a heavy rain probably needs some drainage work.

Grading and drainage are interrelated but separate concepts. The best way to create and ensure good drainage is almost always by proper grading, but there are times when the installation of a subterranean system of drain lines is your only option. When a yard drains as the result of proper grading alone, however, there is nothing to maintain or repair. The lay of the land dictates the flow of the water, as in nature. If you must resort to installing drain lines, you will always need to make sure that the catch basins are kept clear, that the French drain does not become filled with silt, and that an errant shovel doesn't slice through an underground plastic line.

Leveling

Leveling is the process of making the soil surface smooth, but not necessarily flat. Beginning landscapers are very good at leveling, because it is easy both to see and to fix what looks like a problem. They haul truckloads of tiny clods to the dump in an effort to create a lawn as flawless as a billiard table. But leveling is just frosting, and if your cake has fallen flat in the oven, no amount of sprinkles and fancy swirls can fix it. You can have a perfectly level yard that does not drain (because it has been made both smooth *and* flat, but not *graded;* water needs a slope in order to run off). A marsh, such as California's own Central Valley before it was drained, is a naturally occurring example of this landform. And you can have a yard that drains beautifully but is not smooth (think now of the Sierras). But what you *want* is a yard that has been graded, so that it drains, but that is level (i.e., smooth), so that it looks nice and can be used. Something like the foothills, or even the coastal range.

LEVELED, BUT NOT GRADED
TO DRAIN

GRADED TO DRAIN,
BUT NOT LEVELED

So make sure your yard drains before you go to the effort of leveling it. In fact, leveling should only be done at the very end of your project, right before the soil surface is to be covered by sod or mulch.

Before we can talk meaningfully about grading, drainage, and leveling, a few more definitions are in order. These will be somewhat abbreviated, just enough so you can keep up with the discussion.

Swales

A swale is basically a glorified ditch. But whereas a ditch is usually straight-sided and obvious in its intent, a swale is ideally

DITCH

SWALE

graded in such a way that it is barely perceptible to the eye. The creation of slopes and the swales that drain them is an integral part of the grading process.

Drain Lines, French Drains, and Catch Basins

These terms refer to the different components of subterranean drainage systems. Water enters a drain line from a downspout, a French drain, a grate, or a catch basin. A "French drain" is essentially a ditch that is kept open with a perforated pipe surrounded by gravel. A catch basin is a drainage gate with a trap for collecting sediment, the enemy of all drainage systems.

Drain lines slope gently so that water will flow in them. They can terminate at the street, a swale, a storm sewer, a creek, or a sump (a pit filled with gravel). Or a drain line can "daylight" and dump water out onto the ground (preferably far away from a house or a neighbor).

Now that you're armed with these essential definitions, you can navigate the troubled waters of your own private swamp with grace and aplomb.

THINKING LIKE WATER

The trick with grading and drainage is to think like water. What does water want? Water wants any one of three things: to be absorbed, to find the ocean, or to lie stagnant, breeding mosquitoes.

We can increase the water-holding capacity of the soil up to a point, but once the ground is saturated, water will either run off or pool up. To prevent pooling and promote runoff, you need to understand a seemingly simple point: Water only flows downhill. It won't do you any good to put in a swale or a French drain, for example, on the top of a hill. Such devices must be placed in an area where water will naturally collect, such as the base of a slope. You can do everything else by the book, but if you can't think like water, you can't outsmart it. Water acts in accordance with its own rules, not your good intentions.

NEW HOMES AND OLD

Most new homes drain correctly when they are first built. It is only when a hapless homeowner unwittingly interferes with the drainage scheme so carefully worked out by the grading engineer, the city planners, the developer, the builder, and the builder's contractor that there is a problem. So a new homeowner's first job is to avoid impairing the existing drainage scheme. Typically this consists of downspouts hooked up to a drain line to dump at the curb, with swales along the back and sides of the property draining to the front, or, if that's not feasible, to a builder-installed storm drain, and the earth throughout graded to fall away from the house and fence lines.

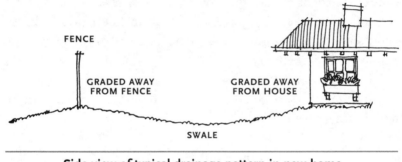

FENCE

GRADED AWAY
FROM FENCE

GRADED AWAY
FROM HOUSE

SWALE

Side view of typical drainage pattern in new home

If your landscape plans call for items that will alter the drainage pattern of your yard, you must make accommodations for the water that will be displaced. So, if you simply must put a brick patio right on top of an existing drain grate, drain the patio down into it, or move the grate and regrade the surrounding soil toward it. Do something to channel water in another way. Don't just cover that grate up. (I've seen this done, and the following winter, you could have raised ducks back there.)

Maybe instead of a grate for a subterranean system, there is just the gentlest of swales down the center of your yard. Careless leveling? Not! Fill that swale up and you'll need flood insurance.

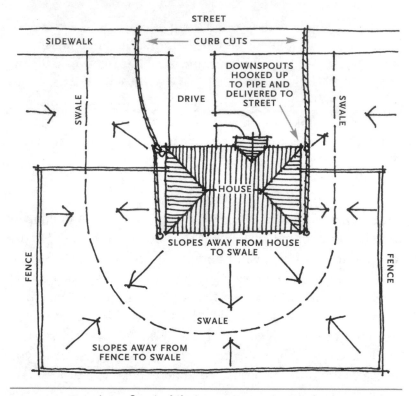

STREET

SIDEWALK

CURB CUTS

DOWNSPOUTS
HOOKED UP
TO PIPE AND
DELIVERED TO
STREET

DRIVE

SWALE

SWALE

HOUSE

FENCE

FENCE

SLOPES AWAY FROM HOUSE
TO SWALE

SWALE

SLOPES AWAY FROM
FENCE TO SWALE

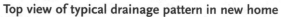

Top view of typical drainage pattern in new home

In older homes, it seems that various forces (clueless construction, heaving tree roots, etc.) conspire over time to create drainage problems where perhaps none existed originally. In these cases, it is not always feasible or desirable to correct problems by means of grading alone. In landscapes with existing features that you wish to preserve—trees, for example—you will be unable to do the amount of soil moving necessary to correct a major drainage problem. In such an instance, you will need to resort to installing underground drain lines.

Whether your home is new or old, first do all your demolition and tear-out before beginning your drainage work. Then, when your yard is as clear and blank as it will ever be, study the lay of the land and envision how it would look (or observe how it does look) in a heavy rainstorm. Your mission is to hasten the journey to the ocean of each drop of water that falls in your yard.

GRADING 101

Water is impeded in its passage in one of two ways: A buildup of earth blocks it, or it rests in a low spot with no way out. To correct the first problem, you remove soil; to correct the second, you add soil. What you will find in most yards is that the high spots equal the low ones, so that when you grade, "Matter is neither created nor destroyed." (This is a good thing, since the import or export of large quantities of dirt is expensive, tiring, and thankless.) Sometimes this cut-and-fill process is all you need to do in order to ensure good drainage. (The process will be easier if you soften up the soil first either by soaking it a few days beforehand, or by tilling it, or both; see Chapter 5, Soil Preparation, for some hints on this process.)

Let me warn you, though, that it takes a discriminating eye to do this seemingly simple task of shifting soil from high spots to low. A difference of only an inch or two can mean life or death

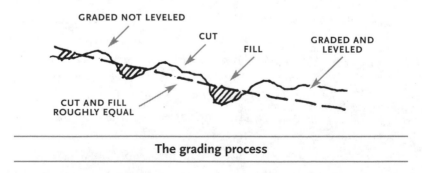

The grading process

to a plant that has the misfortune of growing in clay. Like the ability to spell, a talent for grading seems to be more innate than learnable. Believe me, I have tried teaching countless employees over the years to see subtle variations in topography, and I still end up directly supervising the movement of each shovel myself.

SLIPPERY SLOPES

Surfaces must also slope in order to drain. For very flat, level surfaces, such as smooth concrete, the slope can be so little as to be nearly imperceptible (1 to 2 percent, or one to two feet of drop per one hundred linear feet). The rougher the surface, the more slope is needed to ensure that water will flow across it. Lawns meant for playing, for example, are usually sloped at 2 to 3 percent. This means that for every one hundred feet, the grade must drop two or three feet.

How much slope is too much? It depends primarily on your soil type. Sandy, uncompacted soils erode more readily than compacted clays. To steal the title of a favorite Wallace Stegner book, the permissible slope of different materials is dictated by their "angle of repose"—that is, the angle at which they cease moving (and begin to "repose"). Generally speaking, though, no hill is stable at greater than a 100 percent slope (equal rise for every run, or a forty-five-degree angle). So for that same one hundred feet of horizontal distance, you would have one hundred feed of vertical drop. Any slope more than 50 percent is a strong candidate for a retaining wall, or at the very least, erosion-control measures such as jute netting and stabilizing plantings. (For more on such measures, see "Hillsides" in Chapter 7, Planting.)

PICKS, SHOVELS, AND RAKES

If your ground is very hard, soak and then till it before you start trying to grade it (see "Rototilling," in Chapter 5, Soil Preparation). Begin grading at the "edges" of your property—normally, the walls of your house, the edge of the sidewalk and drive, and your fence lines. Because the grade of these items cannot be changed, they are the givens in your grading equation. When you are grading, it's important to start at a fixed point and then work your way into areas in which the soil level can be made either higher or lower without much consequence. If you start in the middle of your yard, you could end up at the edges with too much or too little soil, and then you'd have to redo all your hard work. And that's not why you bought this book, is it?

Begin by making sure that the earth is at the correct grade (height) at these fixed points. The dirt should be two or three inches lower than any untreated wood surfaces such as fence boards, and at least four inches (and six is better) from the siding or stucco of your house. (You didn't know this? Neither did I, and the $5,000 worth of work I neglected to do when I bought my first house tripled when I sold it three years later. Ignorance was not bliss.)

Your grade should be about three inches lower than the height of your driveways, patios, and sidewalks in areas that are to be mulched, and about an inch and a half lower in areas to be turfed, to accommodate these materials (see illustrations on next page). Of course, if you will be bringing in topsoil or amending the soil with compost (see Chapter 5, Soil Preparation), I wouldn't get out a measuring tape yet; just be aware that you need to accommodate more material than is currently there.

The next step is to slope your land away from those same fixed edges (house, fence lines, patio, etc.) so that water does not drain onto, into, or under them. Work your way with shovel and rake, and perhaps even pick and digging bar, along the perimeter of your yard. You are creating (or re-creating, as the case may be) slopes to lead the water toward a dispersal point (the street, or a creek, say) or a collection point such as a swale, French drain, or grate. All slopes in your yard, both gentle and steep, *must* lead to such designated destinations.

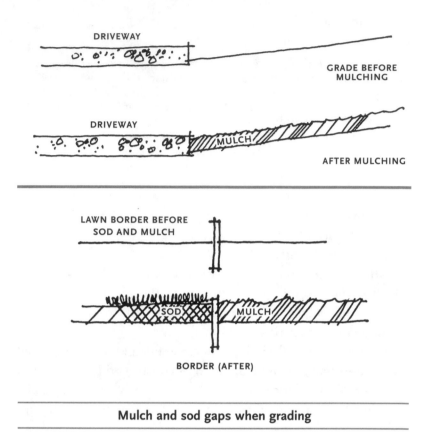

DRIVEWAY

GRADE BEFORE
MULCHING

DRIVEWAY

MULCH

AFTER MULCHING

LAWN BORDER BEFORE
SOD AND MULCH

SOD   MULCH

BORDER (AFTER)

Mulch and sod gaps when grading

We'll talk more about French drains and grates under "Subterranean Systems," but for now we're still just making swales. Do be aware that the more water the swale must carry, the bigger it must be. In some cases, a drainage swale might be so large that it is best to disguise it as a dry creek bed (see "Dry Creek Beds" in Chapter 3). This is also the time to be creating your berms, if any. Soil excavated for swales or general grading can be deposited where your berms will go. And of course, your berms will slope into your swales.

Not only must slopes drain into swales, but the swale itself must also drain, or you will have created a moat. In very flat yards, you must be careful not to begin your swale too deep, or you will use up all your available slope before you've reached the destination. What will happen if the depth of your swale is lower in any one place than at the end is that you will have created a low area with no outlet. So be stingy with the amount of fall you allow in any given portion of your swale, unless you have plenty of height differential from one end of the yard to another. You may even want to "shoot some grades" (measure the relative heights, as discussed in Chapter 2) to ensure adequate fall from one end of the swale to another before you begin.

Because a French drain is just a swale filled in with a pipe and rock, these same principles apply to its construction as well. (And to plain drain lines too, although because the water is contained in a pipe you can generally get away with a few dips and humps without losing efficacy, provided the end of the line is lower than the beginning.)

You can have more than one swale. In large or complex yards, you may have multiple drainage channels leading to a single collection point or to many. You also do not have to put a single swale down the

QUICK TIP

An exception to the slope-to-swale rule can apply on large hillside properties where one home site is simply higher than (and drains onto) the next. In these cases, you are fine if you leave the grade as is. But the moment you collect water in a pipe, ditch, or swale, you are not allowed to divert it to your neighbor's property. In most cases, unless you have a lot of land, it's best to try to contain the water from your property *on* your property, or divert it to an approved outlet such as the street.

QUICK TIP

When you think you are done with your basic ditch, run water from your highest point to see if it does indeed reach its destination. If you ever played in the dirt when you were a kid, you know what comes next. Fill and dig out till the flow is uniform throughout. Then, when your ditch runs as it should, turn it into a swale by grading away the sides so they won't erode back down into your passageway. If the drainage channel is to become a drain line or a French drain, you can leave the sides straight and follow the instructions for a French drain (see page 111).

center of your yard. As long as you can divert water where you need it to go, you can put your swale or swales almost anywhere. This is especially important when you want the center of your yard to be mostly flat.

SUBTERRANEAN SYSTEMS

Every surface in your yard that is impermeable to water creates instant runoff. Your roof, your patio, and even an overflowing pond can shed great volumes of water that need to be disposed of in a hurry. In these cases, it is sometimes best to collect water from high-runoff areas in gutters, downspouts, and catch basins, put it in a pipe, and shoot it out to the street or creek.

Another case where you'll want to install an underground system is when it would simply be too much work to reconfigure the lay of the land in your yard to make it shed water naturally. In these instances, it will be easier to grade your yard toward several existing or designated low spots, which are then hooked up to a drain line to take the water away.

It is fairly easy to figure out where your collection points will be. You'll want to hook up each downspout and any unsolvable low spots throughout the yard. The downspouts will be connected directly to the drain line (and do use the special little downspout adapters they sell). Water in the low spots will enter the drain line from French drains, grates, or catch basins.

You'll want to make sure that, just as for swales, the water collection points at the beginning of your line aren't lower than those farther along or lower than the drain line itself, or water will not be able to drain from them. (Remember, it can't flow uphill, much as you might need it to!)

Selecting the dispersion point(s) for the water you have collected may take a little ingenuity. In country properties, it may be enough to get the water away from the house and let it soak into the pasture and eventually find its way to the creek. But urban and suburban lots must usually be drained out to the street. If there is a sidewalk but no "curb cut" (a sleeve inserted under the sidewalk to which you can attach your line so that it empties into the gutter), you may need to create one, which usually requires a permit. (You could take your chances and daylight your pipe right at the sidewalk, allowing water to flow over the walk, but this tactic could create a hazardous situation, so I don't recommend it.)

Dig the trenches for your drain lines as you would your swales, beginning at the highest point and conserving the fall along the run so that it can be apportioned as you need it. With any drain line or swale, sediment and debris will collect at the lowest spots. In drain lines, either solid or French, material will fill the pipe or trench in these low spots, decreasing the carrying capacity of the system. That's why it's important to keep the slope of your trenches even so that debris and sediment will be flushed out in the flow of the water.

DEBRIS BLOCKING WATER IN A LOW POINT OF A DRAIN LINE

For solid drain lines, your trenches need to be only as wide as your pipe. (For tips on digging your drain lines, see "Trenching" in Chapter 6, Irrigation Systems.) If yours is a large yard with good access, it may be worthwhile to invest in renting a trencher.

Because the water in drain lines flows by gravity, not pressure, make sure all junctions are in the shape of a Y, not a T (see illustration on next page). Do the Quick Tip hose test described on page 108 before deciding that your trench is finished.

Use corrugated three- or four-inch drain line (that flexible, ribbed black pipe; leave installing rigid drain lines to the professionals). For regular (not French) drain lines, you must use the solid (not perforated) type, since your goal is to send water

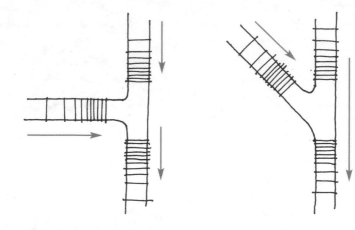

WRONG "T"
(MORE LIKELY TO GET CLOGGED)

RIGHT "Y"
(ENCHANCES DOWNHILL FLOW)

along the line, not to disperse or collect it. Buy the appropriate couplings, Y's, end caps, and grates you think you'll need, and assemble the drain line so that it all fits together. Use grates only where you are certain sediment from erosion will not be a problem (in a lawn, or to drain concrete); use catch basins everywhere else.

QUICK TIP

Before you backfill, test your system once more, and, more important, photograph your lines. You'd be surprised how easy it is to forget where you ran them later, as you're trenching for your irrigation or digging planting holes. And, unlike PVC irrigation pipe, corrugated drainline is easy to slice through with an errant shovel.

FRENCH DRAINS

French drains are particularly suitable for draining large, and especially linear, collection areas. (An example of a linear area would be the base of a retaining wall, or along one side of a house.) Dig whatever ditch you need to drain the area. Follow the same guidelines as for digging a swale, except that the sides can stay straight. Your French drain will work only as well as your ditch does, so you'll want to give it the hose test when you think you are done, making sure again that your slope is even and continuous. Dig your ditch deep enough and wide enough to accommodate a three- or four-inch pipe and some surrounding gravel: at least eight inches deep and as wide. Unless you anticipate huge amounts of runoff, three-inch corrugated perforated pipe—the kind with the slits in it—is fine. If you can find the kind already wrapped in filter fabric, you will save yourself a lot of grief. If not, buy some fabric too.

Line the ditch with fabric, lay the pipe in it, and then wrap the fabric over the top of the pipe and cover it all with three-quarter-inch or so drain rock. You can also line both pipe *and* trench with filter fabric; sediment is the enemy of French drains and can render them useless in a short period of time if it is allowed to infiltrate and fill in the original ditch.

QUICK TIP

In locations where the French drain will be covered with sod or mulch, lay additional filter fabric over the top of your drain rock to ensure that dirt can't enter the system. French drains in turf areas should be avoided. If you must use one (to drain a low spot in an existing lawn, for example), be sure to put fabric over the top, and in addition cover the drain with at least three and a half inches of soil, or the sod above it will dry out.

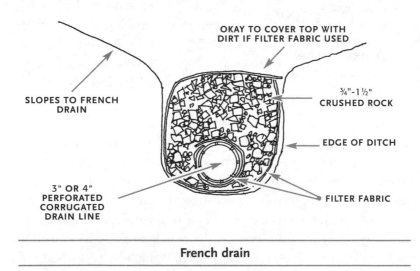

OKAY TO COVER TOP WITH
DIRT IF FILTER FABRIC USED

SLOPES TO FRENCH
DRAIN

¾"-1½"
CRUSHED ROCK

EDGE OF DITCH

3" OR 4"
PERFORATED
CORRUGATED
DRAIN LINE

FILTER FABRIC

French drain

Step on the pipe as you cover it, or gravel will get underneath, raising the pipe out of the trench, and you will have to take everything out and start over.

Connect the French drain to your solid (unperforated) drain line once you're past the low area where you needed to collect

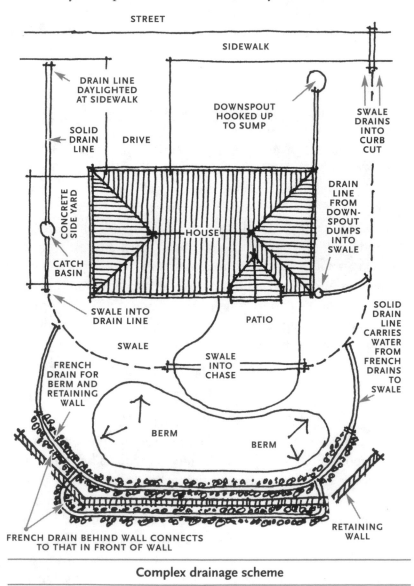

Complex drainage scheme

water. You can also dump water from a French drain into a swale. Although I'm presenting surface grading and underground drainage systems as if they are separate creatures, in reality a comprehensive scheme will always include both species. Slopes can feed into swales, French drains, and/or grates, which then can dump into more swales or drain lines, which can then dump back into catch basins, more drain lines, or even more swales. By studying the lay of your land (and this fine chapter), you should be able to decide when to use a swale and when to opt for a French drain, as well as deciding when you can just grade a problem away and when you need to trench for an underground system.

The process of grading and creating drainage is like the process of writing: You almost never get it right on the first run. You will need to go back and cut a trivial point from one paragraph, and fill in more detail in the next. Everything you do in one part of your yard will affect the rest. In order for a chapter, or a grading scheme, to make sense, it must all flow from one point to another in an unbroken stream. After you've shifted sentences and soil around for a while, though, you'll reach a point where it's good enough. And, come the first storm, or your editor's critique, you'll know whether enough really *was* enough. There is no perfection, only adequacy and inadequacy. So scribble and shovel away till your own perfectionism is sated, and then move on.

THE ART OF GRADING

Most landscape architecture programs require their students to take geology classes, and with good reason. The practice of landscape architecture is essentially the re-creation of natural processes, even in the most obviously manmade environments. Grading is one way in which designers can mimic or reinvent some of these processes as they relate to the form of the earth.

Think of your yard in three dimensions and see if there are opportunities you haven't yet exploited. Have a little fun with your grading. As long as you can make everything drain, there's no reason not to have a sunken patio, or a pavilion on a pinnacle. Use earthen berms to create a sense of enclosure, to block and frame views along a path. A steep drop-off, either created or existing, can be the perfect spot for a waterfall. Lawns don't always have to be flat. When I was a child I used to love visiting my friend Marina, who lived next to a golf course. We'd sneak out at night after all the golfers were gone and roll down the slopes till we were dizzy with glee.

Solving Dire Problems

So far, we have assumed that at one time your yard drained, and that all you have to do now is to restore it to that lost virginal state of innocence. But let us consider the case of a site that was never correctly graded. In such a case as this, you will need a deeper understanding of the grading process, a better understanding of your watery foe, and more expertise than you may care to develop.

I just visited a new home built about two feet from an almost vertical slope rising up behind it. I could not believe that the home had passed inspection, because the slope was not retained, and there was no apparent drainage between it and the house. The first good monsoon of an El Niño year, and that house will be buried in mud like Herculaneum. In a situation like this one, there will be no cunning little swales to shape. What are needed are the big guns of your drainage arsenal. You need engineers and earthmovers, lawyers, and religion. Sorry—if this is your house, I can't help you. Look under "Drainage—Property" in the yellow pages.

But in a more normal but perhaps never-graded yard, the process is much the same as I've described so far. You must grade starting at the edges and send water away from the house in slopes and swales. The main difference is in the amount of soil that may need to be moved. Heavy equipment can be an attractive option in this instance, in which case you may as well hire a professional grading and drainage contractor to operate it, and in fact to do the whole job! If you have to rent equipment, you won't save that much by having your own inexperienced self at the controls.

I once worked in a new home subdivision in which the drainage provided by the builder was woefully inadequate. There simply wasn't enough fall from the back to the front for water to run off. So what everyone did was bring in lots of dirt to raise the level of their back yard. The yard I worked in was surrounded on three sides by neighbors who had already done this. All three neighbors watered their back yards with gay abandon bordering on ecocide. As a result, my hapless customer had algae (yes, *algae*) in *her* yard. Our only recourse was to raise her grade too. No one wants to be the low man (or woman) on the totem pole, or in the neighborhood.

Another time, I did a job in what was called the "Laguna" area east of Sebastopol. Having stupidly studied French in school and not Spanish, I didn't give much thought to what this might mean. Well, I may know what a French drain is, but I had no idea that *laguna* means "lake" in Spanish. This place *had* no downhill I could drain anything to. It was perfectly flat, and whatever water remained after the soil was saturated pretty much stayed right where it fell until it evaporated or was finally absorbed. All I could do was bring in lots and lots of soil and create a series of low islands in what was essentially a vernal swamp. (In the areas between the berms, I planted lots of water-loving riparian plants, which are thriving.)

Enough horror stories? My point is that some drainage problems are insurmountable or will require heroic efforts. But in most cases, there is a solution. Here are the most common problems I see, and what can be done about them.

- *Wet areas at the base of berms or walls.* If possible, grade the soil away in a continuous gentle line until you meet up with a swale. If this can't be done, put in a French drain and connect it to a swale or drain line.

- *Wet areas in the middle of lawns.* A toughie. For a "low spot with no outlet" situation, either you can slowly build up the grade of the soil by adding a thin layer of topsoil every few months and letting the grass grow up through it, or you can just dump on a whole pile of dirt and then resod. For humps that impede the flow of water, you can strip back the sod, remove some soil, replace the grass, and water well until it is reestablished. But for anything large-scale, your best bet is probably to trench through and install a catch basin in the low area (as I noted above, French drains in turf areas are a last resort—they're too disruptive, and the lawn above them dries out too readily). It's easier to insert a drain line than you'd think; just peel the sod back as you trench through it so that you can replace it in exactly the same spot.
- *Water at or under the foundation.* A swale or a French drain next to the house should take care of this. If you suspect the problem is more than just surface water, make your French drain deeper than the bottom of the foundation (if you will still have enough fall) so that it will catch moisture moving through the soil itself, not just runoff.
- *Retaining wall leaning due to water pressure behind it.* Should have put a French drain behind it! (See "Retaining Walls" in Chapter 3, Phasing the Construction.)

WHEN NO SOLUTION IS THE BEST SOLUTION

I had a client in Marin who lived in a house with spectacular views. This was because the house was built into the side of a steep hill. This client had children, too: little boys, three and five. The kids pedaled their Big Wheels with great enthusiasm around the confines of the deck, but clearly it would have been nice for them to have a lawn to frolic on, and a spot of earth to dig in. "Buy another house," I advised. The logistics of designing and constructing steps, landings, and retaining walls in order to create and then access flat, usable ground were such that it would have been a lot easier and cheaper to just move.

I had another pair of clients with a vernal pool. They didn't call it that. In fact, they blacked out the designation "Vernal Pool" on my landscape plan with magic marker, fearful that the authorities would lay claim to the area. Our views on the best use of this area diverged wildly. I saw it as an asset—a sparkling focal point in the wet season, a home to wildlife and unusual plants in the dry months. My customers feared mosquitoes, and didn't want to be kept awake at night by the songs of frogs. They wanted that pool *gone*. They had even gone so far as to order a sample truckload of dirt, just to see how many truckloads they'd need to fill it in.

Thirty cubic yards of fill sounds like a lot of earth, but thirty cubic yards was a fraction of the fraction of what would have been required to fill in their wetland.

Discouraged, these folks looked into ways of draining the area through their neighbor's property. They convinced themselves that the neighbor had once filled in *his* land, blocking the flow from theirs. They argued and wheedled and finally threatened lawsuits, claiming that the pool was a potential health hazard. The neighbor, a farmer in his eighties who had lived there for over thirty years, was flabbergasted at these newly arrived city folks demanding that he fix their "problem." Last I heard, no one was talking to each other, and my former clients had made a new enemy they didn't need.

The pool dried up in the first few warm days of spring. The mosquitoes never even had a chance to hatch. I was out there after it was nearly dry, checking the irrigation to the willows I'd put in, when I saw a damp patch of earth move. Startled, I looked closer and discovered a writhing, wriggling mass of tadpoles desperately seeking the last few puddles of standing water. I scooped the muddy mess into a bucket and took them home to my pond, where frogs are welcome, mosquitoes are controlled with fish, and no one is suing anyone else.

With grading and drainage, sometimes it is better just to go with the flow.

 Chapter 5

Soil Preparation

Making Beautiful Dirt

There is one crucial task that will pay big dividends throughout the life of your garden. Proper soil preparation will inspire even the pokiest plants to grow just a little faster, bloom a little harder, and fight off pests and disease with more conviction.

Preparing your soil for planting doesn't have to be a big mystery. In fact, if you have really good soil, you may not need to do much more than grade it. Your soil type and condition will largely determine how extensive your efforts to improve it need to be.

When my husband and I moved to our almost-an-acre in Sebastopol, one of the first things that happened was that my dog Dingding died suddenly in an accident. I cried and cried as we dug a big hole to bury him. But even through my tears, I couldn't help noticing what wonderful soil we had. Three feet down, it still had the color and consistency of fudge. "Wow," I thought, "we are going to have a great garden here." And we do.

If your soil reminds you more of rocky road or chewing gum than fudge, read on . . .

SOIL TYPES

Let me begin by telling you: *Everyone* thinks they have the worst soil in the world. Even those blessed with sandy loam the color of a caffè latte will swear they have never seen such terrible soil, that it is "hard as a rock." But in most cases, their soil is just really dry. The same soil that bends a digging bar and sneers at a pickax in August will let a shovel cut through it like butter after the first couple of rains.

Here is a little secret. Your soil does not have to look anything like the "soil" you buy in bags at the nursery in order to be wonderfully fertile and productive. The very availability of packaged soil has set up impossibly high standards of soil quality for the home gardener. Like an airbrushed centerfold, the stuff just isn't for real. Real soil is like a real woman: a little lumpy in places, with an occasional obstinate boulder or two . . . and more flinty minerals than fluffy additives.

The soil types that will give you big problems fall into three different categories: extremely sandy, extreme clayey, and extremely rocky.

Sandy soils, although very easy to work with, are hard to manage after planting, because they don't retain either water or nutrients very well. They also attract lots of gophers and moles.

Clay soils are frustrating both to work and to manage. Really heavy clay soils seem to have a window of about a day between their two extremes; they are sticky and gummy when wet, and impenetrably hard when dry. They can prove deadly to a lot of plants, not because they are infertile (in fact, clay soils are often *more* fertile than sandy ones), but because they drain so poorly. With clay soils, you cannot afford to be cavalier about drainage. Since the tight-packed soil particles drain so slowly, your surface grading and drainage must be impeccable. Even then, some plants (those the *Sunset Western Garden Book* describes with the phrase "must have good drainage") will still be a poor bet. With heavy clay soils, it is best to amend deeply, generously, and often; plant judiciously; water intelligently; and pray fervently.

Here's the sixty-second soil test. Get the soil wet. Loosen it up a bit. Pick some up and squeeze it. Can you make it into a little ball? Or does it all collapse the minute you open your hand? Does it sort of make a ball and then collapse, or does it make a ball firm enough to play ping-pong with? The firmer the ball, the more clay. No cohesiveness at all indicates sand. Anything in between these two extremes we'll call loam.

The only problem with rocky soils is that they are such a pain to work with. If the rocks are large and numerous enough, the soil cannot be tilled, trenching is a nightmare, and each planting hole becomes an exercise in frustration. We've done jobs where the hole for a twenty-four-inch boxed tree has had to be moved three times before we found a sufficiently rock-free spot to accommodate the root ball.

Yet rocky soils are often quite fertile. Just because you go nuts trying to trench or excavate in the stuff, don't assume your plants will have an equally hard time of it. It amazes me how many people think plants can't grow in rocky soil. They go to Herculean efforts to remove their rocks, filtering all their soil through a mesh screen to create something resembling the potting soil ideal . . . while up in the Sierras, whole pine trees survive quite happily on a couple of gallons of decomposed granite lodged between two boulders.

Logistically, tree roots present the same problems as rocks. Trying to till in root-infested areas can be as dangerous as it is futile. In addition, the feeder roots of most trees lie within the first foot to foot and a half of soil, so activities such as tilling and trenching can severely impact a tree's health. Often it's best to improve the soil around each plant rather than attempting to work the soil throughout the entire drip line of mature trees. Another good alternative is to plant in berms of topsoil.

There are books, classes, careers, and whole industries all focused on the fine distinctions between clays, sands, and loams, between a loamy sand and a sandy loam, a loamy clay and a clayey loam, but for our purposes, you will have a problem only if you have nearly pure sand or pure clay (or nearly pure rock or roots).

If you prefer method to your madness, you can always get your soil professionally tested. (Call your county ag commissioner or Master Gardener's office for a list of places.) You will receive a report detailing your soil's classification and its percentages of organic matter, nitrogen, potassium, phosphorus, and lesser nutrients.

What are some telltale signs that your soil may be less than perfect? The main thing that gives me cause to pause is a lack of weeds.

The presence of healthy weeds indicates the potential to grow equally healthy plants. Weeds, after all, are just the plants you don't want. The distinction between a "nasty weed" and a "lovely plant I just paid fifty dollars for" is a cultural one, not a botanical one.

Usually, if there are no weeds, or only very stunted weeds, around a new home, it means that the topsoil was scraped off during the grading for the site, and what you have now is infertile subsoil. (If your home is *very* new, it can simply be that it hasn't rained since the house was built and the land was graded.)

With an older home, a lack of weeds can indicate high maintenance standards in the neighborhood—that is, no one lets their weeds go to seed. Or there could be lots of leaf litter acting as mulch. Or, heaven forbid, the last owner may have sterilized the place. You'll want to do a little detective work before you assume that the soil itself has a problem.

DRAINAGE WOES

Poor drainage can be related to soil type (typically, heavy clays) or to soil conditions (compaction, hardpan, subsurface rock layers). Though the most common impediment to drainage is a high percentage of clay in the soil, you can have a light, porous, sandy soil—a type known to generally drain well—which drains poorly because it is compacted.

A smart home landscaper will dig a few holes throughout the property and fill them with water before planting. If those holes still have standing water in them the next day, you are in big trouble. I'm uneasy if the water takes more than six hours to drain. If this happens, try to find out what the problem is.

If your soil is sandy or loamy, but still your test holes do not drain in a reasonable amount of time, your first approach should be to determine the exact nature of the problem. Is the soil loose, or is it dense? If the soil is dense, your problem is the fairly common one of soil compaction. Any soil type, but especially clays and loams, can become compacted. I mostly see this with newer homes where heavy machinery was driven on the site during construction. The solution is to restore the lost air spaces to the soil. If the compaction is moderate, you may be able to do this by tilling. Severely compacted soil may need to be "ripped" with heavy equipment to a depth of eighteen inches or so. If this is not feasible (a tractor won't *fit* in many back yards), you can always rent a jackhammer to dig your holes. You think I am joking? I wish I were.

If your soil is loose, there is probably an impervious layer (a "hardpan") lower down. Dig down a couple of feet and see if you can find the obstruction. The absence of tall trees in the neighborhood may indicate a layer of hardpan a few feet below the surface. You may need to break through this layer in each hole you dig, or, if the layer is shallow, it may be feasible to till or rip the soil.

If the hole you filled with water takes over six hours to drain for *any* reason, I'd consider importing topsoil, in the form of berms or raised beds.

AMENDMENTS

It would seem to make perfect sense to add sand to clay, or vice versa, to make loam. Wrong! Sand plus clay equals cement. (I could go to great lengths to explain the chemistry and physics of this, which I learned long ago in my Soils class at the JC, but

I've forgotten the details. We'll both just have to take it on faith at this point.)

The way to greatly improve all soils is to incorporate large quantities of organic matter. It seems counterintuitive, but adding organic material to sandy soils helps them retain water, while doing the same to clay soils helps them drain faster. (You lucky loam owners can probably get away without adding anything at all to enhance your soil texture, though even fabulous soils can always be improved upon.)

The unfortunate news about amending soil is that all you can hope for is to improve the top twelve inches or so. You will still have impervious clay or droughty sand as far as your trees and large shrubs are concerned. The reason for this is that most equipment can only effectively cultivate the top foot or so of soil. This is great for small plants such as perennials, annuals, turf grass, and groundcovers, but pretty useless for any plants with roots that go down several feet. In fact, studies have shown that it is best to plant trees directly into the existing soil, without the supposed benefit of any amendments at all. Since they must eventually adapt to this soil, the thinking goes, the sooner they do so, the better.

So even if you amend your soil with organic matter, be aware that doing so will have little consequence for your larger plants. In fact, if your plan does not call for any lawn or small plants at all, I wouldn't bother tilling and amending the entire garden. Just incorporate amendments at each planting hole.

In order to make any lasting difference to your planting medium, you will need to add at least four inches of material throughout your entire yard, and six inches is even better. This is a lot of stuff. In your average new subdivision front or back yard of a couple of thousand square feet, this will

QUICK TIP
To calculate the amount of any bulk materials you will need, multiply the square footage of the area by the number of inches of amendment you want. Divide by 324, and presto, you will have the number of cubic yards you need.

translate into anywhere from twenty-four to thirty-seven cubic yards of compost. In case that still seems like an abstraction, let me tell you that such a pile will take up two or three parking places, and will be about six feet high at its peak.

Fertilizers vs. Conditioners

Let me break down the differences between fertilizers and conditioners this way: Soil is both a medium for anchoring plant roots and the means by which a plant secures its nutrients. In hydroponics, the water is the medium, and nutrients are dissolved in it. In your garden, your soil must promote root growth by being loose and friable, *and* it must supply nutrients to those roots.

Generally speaking, fertilizers supply nutrients, and organic matter such as compost promotes root growth by improving soil texture ("conditioning" the soil). A lot of confusion arises from the fact that organic matter does contain some nutrients, and many organic fertilizers are also high in "roughage." But the primary purpose of compost, say, is to alter soil properties such as water retention and workability. And true organic fertilizers, like chicken manure, for example, are valued for their high percentages of nutrients rather than their conditioning effect on soil texture.

I've been throwing around terms like "amendment" and "compost" and "organic material" as if they were interchangeable, and they almost are. "Amendments" are anything that is added to the soil in order to improve *either* texture or fertility: compost, fertilizer, gypsum, manure, superphosphate, a dead fish . . . "Organic amendments" are anything that was once alive: compost, sawdust, leaves, coffee grounds, manure, that same dead fish. "Inorganic amendments" are mineral or chemical in nature: "chemical" fertilizers, gypsum, fireplace ashes, and so on.

There are relatively few organic amendments used on a large scale to increase soil *fertility*. Animal manures are the one product I can think of that can be bought by the cubic yard instead of the plastic bag. By the same token, inorganic amendments are not often used to improve soil *texture*. Gypsum is the one mineral-based material that is available in bulk form to change soil condition. Most inorganic amendments are fertilizers, not soil conditioners.

Landscape supply places often refer to their organic amendments as "soil conditioners," emphasizing textural improvements over fertility. Typically, they will sell several types of these products, depending upon what is locally available and thus cost effective. Most will sell "compost." Unlike the stuff in the smelly little can under your kitchen sink, commercial compost is usually derived from nonfood sources such as farm or ranch waste products or tree trimmings. And in this day of almost universal curbside pickup of yard waste, you may well be buying back your own lawn clippings and leaves, now conveniently broken down and ready for reuse. (You may find old metal rose labels or shreds of plastic in this compost, evidence of a careless homeowner not unlike yourself!)

So-called "mushroom compost" is essentially very well rotted manure, and it smells like it. (The "mushroom" is thrown in there to divert our attention from what the mushrooms lived on.)

"Nitrogenized sawdust" is exactly what the name implies. Nitrogen has been added to the sawdust to make it break down more quickly. This is important, because if you use organic matter that is not composted (that is, not broken down), it will pull nitrogen from the soil as it breaks down, instead of releasing it, as one would like. So do not imagine that you can save a bundle by getting free sawdust from a cabinet shop. (Besides, you don't want any residues of adhesives, wood preservatives, or other bad stuff.)

Rice hulls are another material sold as a soil conditioner or amendment, a by-product of the vast rice farms of the Central Valley. It, too, should either be composted or fortified with nitrogen.

Do not use materials intended for mulch (ground bark, for example) as amendments, because they are not usually decomposed. Also, avoid the free-manure route, unless you can be sure that it is very well rotted. Fresh manures are "hot" (high in nitrogen), and will burn your plants. Your best bet is to get your organic amendments from a reputable, established landscape supply place. In the larger scheme of things, the money you spend on them will be a small fraction of the total expenses of your project.

"Right" and "Wrong" Fertilizers

There is much debate over the merits of the two broad classes of fertilizers, the so-called chemical fertilizers and the organic ones. At the risk of receiving hate mail from organic gardeners far and wide, I'll let you in on a little-known fact: Your plants can't tell the difference! From a marigold's point of view, nitrates are nitrates, and potassium is potassium. Remember I told you that a weed is just a plant we didn't pay for? Well, "chemical" fertilizers are just fertilizers whose manufacture we disapprove of, for various political and aesthetic reasons. An excess of chicken manure—a high-nitrogen organic fertilizer!—has poisoned wells all over Petaluma with nitrates. Yes, these are the same nitrates found in the evil chemical fertilizers. You may approve or disapprove of the means by which various fertilizers are made available to us—through petrochemical manufacture, or cycled through the digestive tracts, bones, and blood of animals—but I can guarantee you, your tomato will be equally pleased with either.

From the plant's point of view, the most significant difference among fertilizers is not how they are produced, but the rate at which they release their nutrients. If nutrients are released more quickly than the plant can take them up, they can leach into the water supply. This can be a problem with nitrogen, especially, because it is highly soluble. The real benefit of organic fertilizers is that most of them release nutrients very slowly, at a rate more commensurate with a plant's needs.

Chances are, nitrogen is going to be the element your plants will need the most of and which your soil will have the least of. This is not unrelated to the fact that it moves through the soil so easily. So it is a good idea to add a slow-release nitrogen source— either a slow-release packaged fertilizer, or manure-based compost—to your soil before planting.

The problem with phosphorus and potassium is that, unlike nitrogen, they move very slowly if at all through the soil, making it difficult to get them to the root zone after planting. So use them now, while it is easy to put them where they'll be needed.

> **QUICK TIP**
>
> The easiest thing to do to cover all your bases is to buy a well-balanced, slow-release, all-purpose fertilizer containing all three major nutrients: nitrogen (N), phosphorus (P), and potassium (K). The numbers on the bag refer to the percentages of each of these three major nutrients, in that order; so 16-16-16 would be good, or 20-20-20, or even 20-10-10. Or, if you prefer to use naturally derived plant food, you can apply bone meal, blood meal, cottonseed meal, bat guano, or whatever, until you have achieved a well-balanced ratio of available nutrients.

ROTOTILLING

There are only two reasons to rototill your yard. One is to fluff up compacted soil, making it easier to dig and grade. The other is to make the soil able to incorporate amendments.

Of course, if your site is on a steep slope, or your ground is too rocky or root-filled, you will be able to improve your soil only on a plant-by-plant basis, because you won't be *able* to rototill. To incorporate amendments into your soil as a whole, though, you will want to till, spread your materials, and then till again. That way, the tilling is broken down into two parts: the groundbreaking and the mixing. You want to till as deeply as you can *before* your amendments are spread, because afterwards there will be so much stuff that all your tiller will be able to do is to mix it up together.

Don't even think of trying to dig up your yard by hand unless you live in a condo, or suffer from incurable masochism, or have the boundless energy of a border collie. This is not the time to forsake modern technology. I mean, why stop at the shovel? Why not use a pointed wooden stick, or better yet, your bare hands?

Unless your yard is very small, you will be better off renting a rear-tine tiller than a front-tine one. They are less maneuverable, but much easier on the operator. They also break up the ground more quickly, and till a wider swath, than front-tine models. Front-tine tillers, however, seem to do a better job of incorporating amendments into previously tilled soil. So if you need to rent a machine twice, once before and once after bringing in the compost, use a rear tine and then a front tine tiller. And if your area is large enough, and you can get one onto your property, your best bet is to rent a tractor with a rotovator (a tiller attachment). I think any area over a third of an acre, without too many obstructions, would justify using a tractor.

QUICK TIP

Before you till, be sure to locate all underground utilities (see "Sources" at the back of the book for tollfree number) and determine their depth. If there is any danger at all of hitting a leach, gas, electrical, cable, or water line, mark the area well and turn over that area and about three feet on either side of it by hand.

The importance of soil moisture in maintaining your sanity during this phase of the landscaping project cannot be overemphasized. Trying to rototill in hard, dry soil will tire you out more quickly than just about any landscape work you do. The machine will buck and cavort, the dust will choke and annoy, and after all that, you'll find you've barely scratched the surface. Plus, you can really hurt yourself trying to till close to the house or a fence if you can't control the machine. What you want to do is soak the area well a few days beforehand.

Sandy soils can be watered deeply two or three days before

tilling. With heavy clay soils, it's best to thoroughly soak the entire area to be tilled at least a week before (for a summer project). If you have already installed overhead irrigation, run each station for an hour or two, using multiple start times if runoff is a problem. If you're watering by hand, you will want to move the sprinkler around and leave it on each placement for an hour or two. Test the soil moisture over the next few days by digging down with a shovel in a couple of different places. With clay soils, you will have a window of about fifteen minutes between "too gooey to work" and "too hard to penetrate."

QUICK TIP

Till in at least two directions, the second at right angles to the first, so there are no missed areas. With hard ground, you will need to make many passes. Go as deeply as you can.

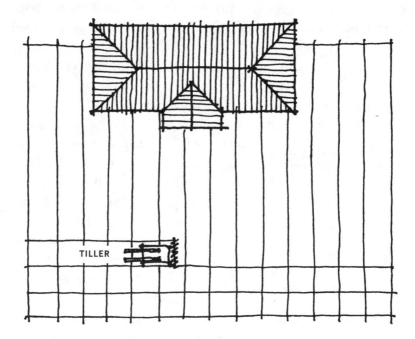

Tilling in two directions

THE TOPSOIL ALTERNATIVE

If you have *really* bad clay, or more rocks and tree roots than workable soil, or unsolvable drainage issues, then your only solution may be to bring in topsoil.

When I say "topsoil," I do not mean those bags of potting soil I mentioned earlier. I mean that material that your local landscape supply outfit sells as "amended loam," or even "amended topsoil." You do not want unamended topsoil, unless you are using it for fill or really extensive berms, where it might be cost effective to amend the top twelve inches yourself. If you buy unamended topsoil, it can actually be almost sterile. Around where I live, the topsoil is dredged from floodplains, and contains no organic matter whatsoever unless it is mixed in.

On the other hand, there are topsoil mixes with too much organic matter. Beware any "soil" that feels very light and appears hardly different from the compost in the neighboring bin. While they're a joy to wheel around in the barrow, these soils will quickly break down until only the small amount of mineral content is left behind. I've seen raised beds filled with overly light topsoil whose soil level sank so much in just one year that they had to be refilled.

Some establishments will sell a variety of specially mixed topsoils, each intended for a different target plant or use. For example, a "planter mix" will perform best in containers, an acid mix will be geared toward acid-loving plants such as camellias and rhododendrons, and so on. Specialty mixes make a lot of

---

QUICK TIP

When bringing in organic matter, begin dumping material at the farthest point from the pile, so you don't have to push a heavily laden wheelbarrow through previously deposited mounds of soft compost. The best way to distribute material evenly is to divide both pile and yard in half and then in half again. Then put that amount of the pile onto that amount of the yard, and you'll be able to gauge your distribution. Otherwise, you will have to steal material from areas where you were too generous, or go back and add more to thin areas, trying to finish off the pile.

sense if you have more than an area or two that will need special treatment. Otherwise, you can always add your own amendments to your basic topsoil; for example, you can add peat moss to acidify a portion of your base topsoil for a small acid-loving shade garden.

There are two pitfalls to avoid in using topsoil. Both stem from the misconception that it is desirable—or even possible—to manipulate nature radically and successfully to our own ends. If you have difficult soil, you will always have difficult soil, deep down. All you can really hope for is to *cheat* a little.

First, you do *not* want to remove all your native soil, no matter how uncooperative it has been. Unless you can find someone who will accept it as clean fill, the dump fees alone will break your budget. If you cannot get equipment in, you will spend countless precious hours at the most backbreaking, thankless, pointless toil you can imagine. The only time I ever excavate and remove soil is if it is badly infested with Bermuda grass. In all other situations, simply design your yard to take into account the fact that you will be adding dirt. Remember the lazy landscaper's operating premise: Work with what you've got.

QUICK TIP

I almost always use a couple of inches of topsoil when I'm putting in a new lawn, even if the native soil is great or has already been amended, just because it makes the scrupulous final grading and leveling so much easier. Instead of raking up endless piles of clods, which then must be dumped, just cover the roughly graded original soil with clodless topsoil. Bring it in after all the borders, irrigation, and rough grading are done, right before you're ready to seed or sod. You can just sweep a rake over the area and presto! You're ready to roll.

The second pitfall stems from the same obsessive mindset. You do *not* need to create a uniform depth of, say, twelve inches of topsoil throughout your whole yard. I have actually done this, building two-by-twelve header boards at the fence lines to retain the new grade, but it was a huge waste of my time and someone else's money.

When you're opting for topsoil, the idea is to get creative. Chances are your plan will call for paths and lawns, planting areas and sitting areas. Lawns and small-scale groundcovers need only about four inches of good soil. Okay, six inches if you are feeling generous. Walkways and sitting areas need none. Trees and major shrubs won't benefit from any amount of soil it would be feasible to provide for them, so select varieties that will tolerate your native soil. That leaves us with the roses and the perennials, the cutting garden and the herbs. These will all be quite thrilled with six to eighteen inches of friable soil.

What I like to do, because it adds interest, is to create low, very gently sloping berms. The larger the berm, the higher you can make the highest point or points of it. The important thing is that the slope of the sides not be so steep, the berms so humped and rounded, that the beholder thinks she's landed at a Scandia Fun Center.

Creating berms in the landscape will affect your drainage patterns, so design them so that they drain into your swales, as

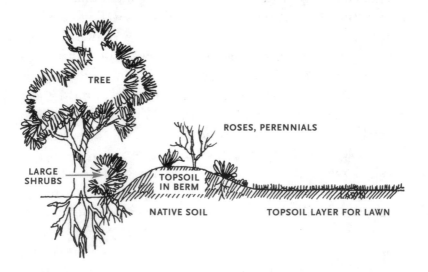

Using topsoil for shallow-rooted plants in berms

mentioned in the previous chapter. The tops of berms will be drier than the bottoms, so if you're using overhead irrigation you may want to site your heads accordingly. Also, I try to use water-loving plants such as irises and red-stemmed dogwoods at the base of a berm.

I am frequently asked whether berms will wash away. The answer is "No more so than the rest of the landscape, if they are mulched after planting and the slope is gentle." I am also asked if they will settle. Yes, depending on how much biodegradable organic material is in the topsoil mix. But do not compact them, since one of the major benefits (a nice fluffy planting medium) will then be lost. Just make them a little higher, say twenty percent, than you want them to be in the long run.

Design your berms around the grade of any existing plants, especially trees. Remember, to bury a tree even as little as an inch or two is to risk losing it to crown and root rot.

Using commercially prepared topsoil instead of your native soil has both advantages and disadvantages. The biggest advantage, of course, is the ease of handling a medium that has been aerated, amended, and screened for your shoveling ease. It is easier to grade and easier to dig. Easier to trench through. Easier to move. All that tiring rake and shovel work is just *easier*.

There are some disadvantages to using imported topsoil, however. Mention imported topsoil to anyone with the tiniest smattering of horticultural expertise, and chances are that he or she will begin to lecture you earnestly on the dreaded soil-interface problem. So, let me beat them to it.

When two unlike soils meet, water will not drain well through them. Even if you had a layer of clay above sand, the water would drain through the clay and then be held up at the sand layer. Yes, I know this seems backwards. So our brilliant plan of abandoning your poorly draining clay soil in favor of nice fluffy topsoil is for naught; you may end up with soggy topsoil on top of dry adobe. What you will learn in any soils class is that you must create a mixed layer between two unlike soil types, to facilitate the passage of water between them. And while I have witnessed the dreaded interface problem only in classroom slide shows, I still dutifully create a transition layer when the topsoil I buy varies greatly from the soil I'm dumping it on.

The only other disadvantage does seem to be the moral angle. I'm not sure why it feels wrong to buy good dirt instead of making your own. After all, I buy frozen burritos and clothes made undoubtedly in factories instead of with my own needle, and I am writing this on a lovely new computer instead of longhand on parchment with ink from dried bugs . . . I guess my twenty-first-century technophilia is improbably balanced with a touch of pagan earth worship, and it just seems a bit disrespectful to Mother Nature to turn our nose up at her best efforts, however sorry the results.

# Chapter 6

Irrigation Systems

Brains Plus Brawn

I t's no coincidence that there is only one letter's difference
between "irrigation" and "irritation." If you have ever tried
to reason with a funky sprinkler system, you will know what
I mean. Broken heads spew water like Boboli's fountain; the side
of the house is soaked every time you water the lawn; and the
soil is spongy in one area, parched in another.

The problem with irrigation is that it seems so simple. "How
hard can it be to glue plastic pipe?" wonders the unwary homeowner. And indeed, the physical skills required—trenching, cutting, and yes, gluing—are not difficult. It is the planning and
layout that will make or break a sprinkler system.

Of all the topics in this book, irrigation will be the most difficult to grasp and yet the most rewarding to master. A well-
designed system that has been properly installed with
good-quality parts will pay for itself many times over in years of
trouble-free, labor-saving service. So either take the time to
learn this craft properly, or hire a well-qualified professional.
(See "Hiring Pros" in Chapter 1, Planning Your Project.)

If you decide to install your own irrigation, I strongly recommend that you get a professional plan if at all possible. Most
certified irrigation designers are pretty pricey for the small
homeowner, but would be an excellent investment for any
homeowner with more than a third of an acre or so. Alterna-
tively, many commercial irrigation supply places will do designs

for free or for very little if you buy all your materials from them. In addition, they will usually pull all the parts and materials you'll need (thus saving you many tedious hours of poring over boxes of look-alike fittings, as well as countless return trips for the ones you forgot).

I also suggest that you pick up a pamphlet on irrigation design and installation from the self-help section of a big chain hardware store, or from an irrigation supply place geared toward the homeowner. It will cover a lot of the basics not dealt with here, will give you an alternative reference to help you understand this one, and will present a lot of handy charts in a compact form.

Plan on buying your parts from an irrigation supply house geared toward the professional installer. Though they won't hold your hand every step of the way, you can be assured that their advice will be a cut above that of the hardware store help. In addition, you simply cannot find good-quality components at hardware or big-box stores. To get professional results, you need to shop where the pros shop.

Lastly, some communities (not many) may want you to get a permit for irrigation work. Check this out.

WHAT PLANTS WANT

The goal of any irrigation system should be to produce happy, hydrated plants in the most efficient manner. From your plants' point of view, the more closely we can replicate the conditions in which they evolved, the better. The problem is that some plants are from the desert, some from swamps, and some from mountaintops. If these plants are all mixed together in the same bed, it will be almost impossible to give each of them the right amount of water. So the first thing you need to think about when designing your irrigation system is to make sure that your plants are grouped into hydrozones.

Hydrozones are simply areas of the landscape in which all the plants have similar water needs. For example, you may have a moisture-loving woodland garden under thirsty redwoods and drought-tolerant sun-worshippers on a rocky slope. These hydrozones should have separate irrigation so they can be watered independently of one another.

Efficiency is an irrigator's next concern. Water must be evenly applied to the area to be irrigated. A system that dumps copious amounts of water in one area while barely misting another will never operate satisfactorily, because it will have to be run for such a long time in order to sufficiently wet the drier area that the wetter ones will be swamped. So you want to design your system to distribute water uniformly.

Efficiency also means supplying plants with the least amount of water necessary for healthy growth. Everyone knows that plants need water. What many do not realize is that plants also need oxygen. Especially in the root zone. I can't tell you how many yards I've seen where the timer had reverted to its default setting—watering every station every day—without the home-owner realizing that this was undesirable. Even in green, green England it doesn't rain *every* day. If more people watered correctly (deep, infrequent soakings, as opposed to a daily spritz), both their plants and our planet would be healthier.

TO DRIP OR TO SPRAY?

Pick up the Home and Garden section of any newspaper in California and chances are you will find an article singing the praises of drip irrigation. Drip systems, we are told, are the only responsible, effective way to water plants. Talk to any landscape maintenance contractor, however, and you will hear a different tune. Drip systems are temporary irrigation, impossible to maintain and difficult to expand. Which song should *you* sing?

If you have lawn areas to irrigate, of course, you will be watering overhead. But what about your plants? Let us weigh the pros and cons of drip versus overhead watering.

What is drip irrigation? A drip system delivers water to the root zone of your plants via "emitters" installed along a length of half-inch or so tubing that snakes throughout your yard. It is fast, cheap, and easy to install. In sparsely planted areas, it uses much less water than overhead irrigation systems in which the entire soil surface is wetted, and it reduces weed growth between plants because only the soil at each emitter gets water.

However, drip systems have several serious drawbacks not apparent to the casual observer. Although they work well in newly planted landscapes, as the plants grow and their root system expands, more emitters must be added. If they are not, the plants will put on a flush of growth each spring, while there is still plenty of moisture in the soil from winter rains, but will then wilt and die back as this reserve is depleted and they must depend on a small damp spot from a single emitter to sustain them. So unless you are prepared to expand your system at least once a year, your larger plants will quickly outgrow it.

Furthermore, in densely planted landscapes, if the conscientious homeowner ensures that emitters moisten the entire root zone of all his plantings, he may as well just water overhead. True, there is still the evaporative loss of water to consider, but by watering in the early morning hours when temperatures are low and winds are calm, and by mulching heavily, this loss can be minimized. In addition, your plants will thank you for rinsing off their dusty leaves.

The other big problem with drip systems is that even with careful maintenance and upgrading, they just don't last very long. The emitters get clogged or fly off, the tubing is sliced through by a shovel or chewed in half by gophers and puppies, and before you know it you're not saving water at all. You'd be surprised how much water can flow out of severed half-inch drip tubing.

To add insult to injury, you may not even notice that anything is wrong until a plant or a whole group of plants are already dead. Plants on drip systems seem to die at the drop of a leaf when their water supply is cut off. I think it is because all their roots become concentrated in the area where the emitter is.

Then, since they have not produced a normal, wide-spreading root system, they have a smaller network from which to draw water if their lone supply dries up.

In my opinion, the more closely your irrigation system can approximate natural rainfall, the better your plants will do. If your primary goal is to save water, by all means install a drip system. If you want a beautiful garden, however, consider over-head irrigation and assuage your conscience by not washing your car, by taking three-minute showers, and by only running your washer with a full load. Or campaign against what I call corporate greenswards: the acres upon acres of turf surrounding office buildings in industrial parks upon which no dogs or kids may gambol, no picnickers lunch, no lovers lounge. Now *that* is a waste of water.

Now that I've catalogued the evils of drip systems, let me tell you why nearly every yard I install has one. There are four situations in which drip excels:

- *As temporary irrigation to establish drought-tolerant plantings.* By the time the system begins to fail (in four or five years), the plants will be able to survive without it, and can be watered by hand with a sprinkler once or twice a season. (Drought-tolerant plants only *tolerate* drought. Most of them look best with an occasional deep soaking.)
- *On steep hillsides where erosion and weed growth could be a problem.* But, in such difficult areas, *do* use drought-tolerant plants that will survive the inevitable failure of the system.
- *In sparsely planted areas.* The amount of water you'll save in the spaces between the plants will be significant.
- *Anyplace where overspray from overhead irrigation could be an issue.* Such areas include small or oddly shaped plots as well as areas against or near buildings or other structures (see illustration on next page).

Finally, to use drip in the following situations is to invite disaster:

- *In thickly planted perennial beds.* Every time you cut your plants back to the ground, you'll slice through that spaghetti tubing,

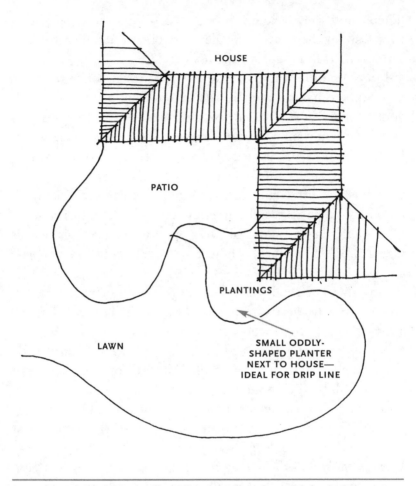

Drip excels in small, oddly shaped areas near the house.

whether you notice it or not, and come summer you'll have dead plants.

- *With big trees.* Whereas a newly planted tree may do just fine with a necklace of emitters along its root ball, within a few years that tree will need lots of water—much more than you can feasibly provide with drip. I soak my young trees from trunk to drip line (the outermost edge of the canopy) for three or four hours several times each summer, using just a hose-end sprinkler.

DESIGNING YOUR SYSTEM

It should take you nearly as much time to *design* your irrigation as it will to put it in. Okay, maybe I'm exaggerating, but the point I want to make is that your design will determine whether your system actually works or not. Believe it or not, it'll take the same amount of time to install a useless system as a functioning one. So hey! spend some time with the calculator and a few spec sheets and develop a plan that'll make you proud. This is the "brain" part of irrigation.

Lines and Stations and Circuits, Oh My!

In most yards you will need a variety of different types of irrigation. Typically, you will have spray, impact, or rotor heads (all types of overhead irrigation) serving your lawn and perhaps the densely planted water-loving plants near the house, plus a drip line or two to pick up outlying less-thirsty plants and the odd areas throughout. Now what?

The first step is to decide how many different lines you will have. Imagine if you didn't have much water in your house (perhaps your pipes are corroded, or you live in the country and your pump is failing) and you tried to take a shower, water the lawn, and run the dishwasher all at once. You'd be huddling under a wispy trickle of water while your dishwasher coughed and sputtered and your sprinkler barely wet an area the size of a cereal bowl.

The same thing will happen to your sprinklers if you try to water your entire yard at once. So we group drip emitters or sprinkler heads (the fixtures that water actually oozes or sprays from) together in a given area, separating them into different "lines" so that we can run one section of the yard at a time. Each drip or spray line is controlled by its own valve (the actual unit that turns the water on and off, comparable to the faucet you use to turn the hose on and off). The timer which controls the operation of these valves refers to each line as a "station," "zone," or even "circuit." Much of the confusion over terminology would be omitted if we could just make up our mind as to whether a line is a zone, a circuit, a valve, or a station (these terms are often used interchangeably), but then how could we professionals dazzle you with our sparkling vocabulary?

Deciding how many lines you need is one of the great challenges of the irrigation designer. It is also the first step, because the valves and mainline supplying the lines are installed before they (the lines) are put in. (The mainline carries water from your existing water supply out to the valves.)

The first way to divide your yard and calculate the number of lines you'll need is to determine the number of hydrozones you have, as I've mentioned before. Since each hydrozone should be watered separately, each will need its own line. You may also want to separate vastly different microclimates within your yard into their own lines (see the section on page 152 titled "Grouping Heads into Lines").

QUICK TIP

Always allow for more lines than you think you will need. I was not joking about the cereal-bowl syndrome. There is nothing more humiliating than to turn on your system for the first time and have the water come out as a limp little umbrella.

The next step is to determine whether there is enough available water at your place to run an entire hydrozone at once, or whether it will need to be further broken down into additional, separate lines. I will begin by talking about drip irrigation systems, since drip is so much more flexible and forgiving than overhead irrigation.

Gallons per Hour: How Many Drip Lines?

In the average urban or suburban residential yard, you could water all your plantings by drip from a single valve, if you wanted to (and if you didn't need to separate the water-lovers from the hydrophobics). Whereas the output of conventional spray heads is measured in gallons per minute, drip emitters are rated by the number of gallons per *hour* they use. With drip lines, frequently it is the length of your run of tubing, rather than the number of emitters, that determines how many different lines will be needed. The loss of pressure over long distances can mean that emitters at the end of the line will have less flow available than those closer to the water source. The longer the run, the fewer emitters you will be able to use, and vice versa. (You could compensate for this by using larger diameter pipe in order to increase flow, but in general I like to stick with half-inch tubing, which is more readily available.)

One way to calculate the number of drip lines you'll need is to count up all the plants you need to water and then figure out how many emitters of what size each will get. Then you can project the total number of gallons per hour (gph) you'll need for your entire system.

If you use a soaker hose, mister heads, or mini-sprinklers in your drip system, you should calculate the gph they will need separately from your emitter lines. Since they use so much more water than emitters, they should be on a separate line from them. I would like to take this opportunity to talk you out of using these products,

QUICK TIP

I use one-gallon-per-hour emitters exclusively rather than mixing emitters with different outputs on one line. If one plant needs more water than the next, I simply give it more emitters. And since it is usually the larger plants that need more moisture, the water is distributed more evenly throughout the root ball with two or more emitters than with one. I also choose one-gallon-per-hour emitters because they have a big enough orifice so that they don't clog, and a small enough one so that you can still put a lot of plants on one line.

ANOTHER QUICK TIP

Don't tell anyone, but I just figure on a single one-gallon-per-hour emitter for each four-inch pot or one-gallon plant, two emitters per five-gallon plant, and four or more for sizes larger than that. You'll need to figure on at least doubling those quantities for future growth.

however. Soaker hoses do have their place, but they clog so easily that they should never be considered as a permanent watering device. (Inline emitters can often be substituted for the same applications and are the least cloggable of components.) And mister heads and those micro-mini-sprinklers were invented by the devil himself. Their wee orifices clog at a moment's notice, their cunning little support stakes can be knocked over by the wag of a dog's tail, and the slightest puff of a breeze will blow their spray pattern off course. Besides, I just don't get it. Isn't the whole point of drip systems to reduce water loss from evaporation?

Once you know how many gph you will need, make a rough estimate of how long your runs will be, keeping in mind that you'll want to loop your half-inch tubing throughout your planting beds. The closer your main half-inch pipe will be to your plants, the less tiny "spaghetti" pipe you'll need. And as you will see when we discuss drip line installation, less pasta is a good thing.

The shorter your runs, the more gallons per hour available to you. For example, using half-inch pipe with runs of two hundred feet or less, you will have about 240 gph to work with; at four hundred feet, pressure loss will reduce your flow to around 160 gph. (Get charts from the irrigation place if you want to calculate this more precisely.) Still, 160 gph allows you eighty five-gallon plants if each plant has two 1-gph emitters. Of course, those plants may need more water as they grow, or you may want to add more plants on down the line, so plan accordingly. If you overdesign your system so that you only use half the gallons per hour available to you, you should be just fine.

If the number of gallons per hour you'll need exceeds the capacity of your pipe over the distances it will have to travel, then plan on splitting the area into two lines, or dividing up your drip line so that the valve is centered in the middle of it. That way, one long run can be broken down into two shorter ones right at the valve, reducing your pressure loss—and loss of available gallonage—accordingly.

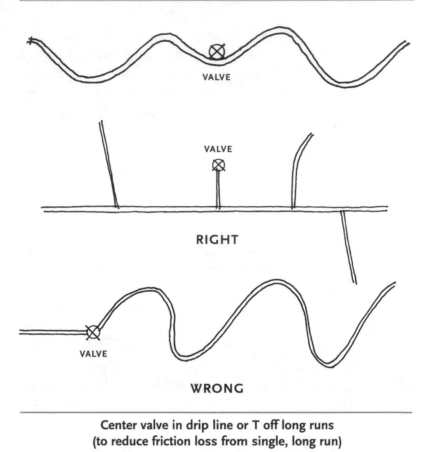

VALVE

VALVE

RIGHT

VALVE

WRONG

Center valve in drip line or T off long runs
(to reduce friction loss from single, long run)

Gallons per Minute: Overhead Spray Lines

In order to calculate how many lines your overhead irrigation
system will require, you must first design the layout of your
heads, so that you can figure out how many gallons per minute
(gpm) they will use. You then divide that figure by the number
of gallons per minute that is available from your water source
(the critical factor for spray lines) to get the number of different
lines you will need.

Sprinkler Heads

While this is not the place for an exhaustive discussion of the
pros and cons of different types of sprinkler heads, I must tell

you that I like impact heads for large areas, and adjustable spray heads for smaller ones, because neither type requires special tools nor an IQ higher than mine to adjust or unclog. I avoid the gear-driven rotors and stream sprays because my clients always lose the cute little tool and the instructions for their adjustment, and then I have to drive forty minutes to perform a simple twenty-second operation. But this is your yard, so choose whatever head seems to suit your situation best. Just don't mix different types of heads on the same line, since the run time needed to produce an equivalent amount of water will vary from one head to the next.

If you use a professional irrigation supply place, ask for the specification sheet for your chosen sprinkler head. This sheet will show how far the water from the head will throw using different nozzles and at different pressures. Measure your water pressure. I find it best to take a reading as close to the valves you will be installing as possible, rather than at the meter or well-head, since changes in elevation will affect your output (measured in psi, or pounds per square inch). You can buy a pressure gauge that threads onto a faucet for about ten dollars. Most residential water pressure is around 40 to 60 psi.

You will notice on the spec sheet that the radius of throw achieved and the gallons per minute used for your head are greatly reduced at very low pressures. At very high pressures, on the other hand, water can spray with such force that it mists rather than rains, increasing evaporative loss. So it may be worthwhile to adjust the pressure regulator for your water supply either up or down to bring your psi into an acceptable range. If you're not sure how to do this, have a plumber or a well-and-pump guy do it for you.

Once you've selected your heads and their nozzles and have calculated their throw (based on your psi), do a rough layout of your landscape plan on the ground, indicating the locations of your lawn, walkways, and planting areas, so that you can place your sprinkler heads accordingly. I never bother doing this on paper, since even the tiniest inaccuracy in your plan can throw everything off. Just go ahead and design your whole overhead irrigation system on the ground, using colored flags to mark the location of each head.

In turf and groundcover areas, start by marking your head locations around the perimeter and then work your way inward. In shrub areas, it is sometimes best to anticipate the eventual

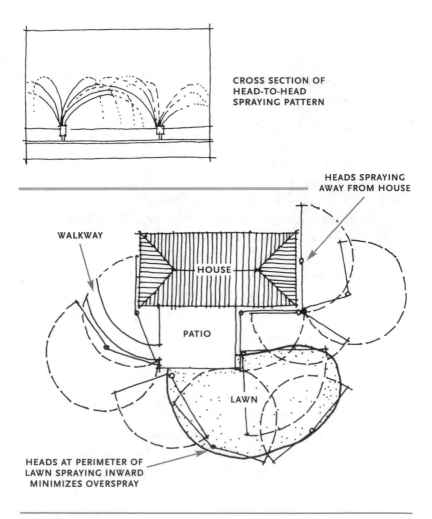

CROSS SECTION OF
HEAD-TO-HEAD
SPRAYING PATTERN

HEADS SPRAYING
AWAY FROM HOUSE

WALKWAY

HOUSE

PATIO

LAWN

HEADS AT PERIMETER OF
LAWN SPRAYING INWARD
MINIMIZES OVERSPRAY

Typical head spacing, with all heads spaced "head to head"

growth of the plants, and begin your heads along a path or some other area where you can be sure the plants will be low and won't grow to block the water. In both cases, avoid placing heads in such a way as to direct water toward nearby buildings. It doesn't take much of a breeze to shift your carefully planned spray pattern a couple of feet in any direction.

On long lines, water may drain out the lowest heads when the system shuts off, creating problem wet areas there. Install check valves "upstream" of the lowest heads to prevent this from happening.

QUICK TIP
Make sure you use head-to-head spacing. That is, the water from one head should reach all the way over to the next head, not just to the perimeter of its spray pattern. If you don't, you will have an uneven distribution of water, resulting in dry areas between your heads. Ideally, every spot will receive water from at least two heads. (See illustration on preceding page.)

How to Measure Your GPM

Once your heads are placed and your nozzles are specified, you can figure out how many lines (and thus, eventually, valves) you will need by adding up all the gallons per minute your entire overhead irrigation system will use, head by head, and dividing it by the gpm available at your water take-off point (the point at which your irrigation system taps into your water supply). This will tell you how many lines for overhead irrigation you will need. In city lots, your water take-off point will be where the water comes into the house from the meter at the street; in rural areas, it is usually best to take your water directly from the pump or holding tank, before it is treated for household use. Both these places will normally sport a faucet from which you can measure both psi and gpm, and which you may later disconnect to use as an entry into your water supply. (More on this in "Installing the Mainline," on page 156.)

Gpm is not the same as pressure. The pounds per square inch of pressure in your system is just one of several factors that influence your flow in gallons per minute. The size of your meter (or the capacity of your pump), and the size of the pipe coming off either of those components is just as important a factor in determining your gpm as the psi is. Almost all municipalities and private water systems have adequate pressure. But sufficient flow—gpm—can be another matter.

The best way to understand the difference between flow (gpm) and pressure is to visualize a high-pressure power washer, the lower Sacramento River, and a giant fire hose. The power washer puts out just a little water at high pressure. The Sacramento puts out a huge amount of water at low pressure (at least in summer). But the fire hose has both flow (a lot of water) *and* pressure.

Most urban water supplies produce between 7 and 15 gallons per minute; in rural areas I rarely encounter more than 20 to 30 gpm. Let's suppose for simplicity's

sake that you have 10 gpm, and that all the heads in your entire landscape will require something like 60 gpm (maybe you have thirty heads and each one uses 2 gpm). You would then need six valves of five heads each. But in reality, you'd be safer to design your system to use less than your available 10 gpm. It would be better to use seven or even eight valves, to compensate for the pressure loss through your pipes and valves. I won't go into much more detail than that, since I would hate for you to toss this nice book into the nearest dumpster in a fit of rage and frustration. Believe me, there are charts and tables and arcane formulas to help you calculate this loss down to the last milliliter—but we'll leave that math for the golf course designers.

Once your heads are laid out, and you know your available gpm, you can calculate which heads to group together into their own lines, and what size valves and timer to use. You can also then decide the location of your valves and the mainline that will supply water to them.

Grouping Heads into Lines

The next step in the process of designing your overhead watering system is to decide which heads to group together in a line. This is not terribly difficult. Of course, you will separate lawns from planting areas. You will also want to minimize the amount of pipe you'll need, so obviously you'll group heads that are near one another, making sure you stay well within your given gpm in any one line. (The total gpm needed will vary from line to line, since the different nozzles you use on each head—to allow for different configurations such as half and full circles—each pull a different gpm.)

If possible, try to group heads within a given mini-microclimate together. For example, if you have one area of the lawn that is sunny and sloping and another that is shady and low, separate those areas into different valves. Then, later, you can

QUICK TIP
Every foot of increase in elevation will decrease your pressure by half a psi; a foot of drop will increase it at the same rate. This is no big deal unless you are talking about major elevation changes (more than a five-foot difference between your highest and lowest heads). Just be aware that changes in psi will affect the gpm available to each head, as well as its throw. Try to group each cluster of heads at a similar elevation into its own valve.

fine-tune your timer settings to accommodate the different water needs of each zone. Now rearrange the colored flags that marked your heads so that each line is designated by its own color.

Mainlines and Manifold Destinies

Once you've divided your irrigated areas into the appropriate lines, you can figure out where your valves go. You will want to group them together in "manifolds" (groups) of two or three valves each. The location of each manifold should be as near as possible to the lines it will serve. There will be other considerations, of course: Avoid putting valves in your lawns or paths, where they will get too much traffic, and if you must use anti-siphon valves (and I will try to talk you out of these shortly), they are best located out of sight, since they are installed above ground.

The "mainline" of your irrigation system is the pipe from your water take-off point to each valve. It is called the mainline because it is like the water main in the street—always under pressure. So if you ever hit it while trenching or digging, you'll definitely know it. ("Lateral lines," like your drip and spray lines, are under pressure only when they are running. You can hit one and not even know it until months later, when you notice that your lawn looks like a map of the world, with brown continents and verdant green oceans.)

Lay out where your mainline will go, connecting your water take-off point to your valve manifolds. Mark it with upside-down paint, stretching a piece of string to make your lines straight, and ensuring that your right angles and forty-five-degree angles are true. PVC pipe does bend a bit, but forcing it around curves is not good, since the stress on the fittings can cause trouble later.

Finally, figure out where you will put your timer. The wires that control the valves will be taped to the underside of your mainline pipe, but unless your timer is located right next to

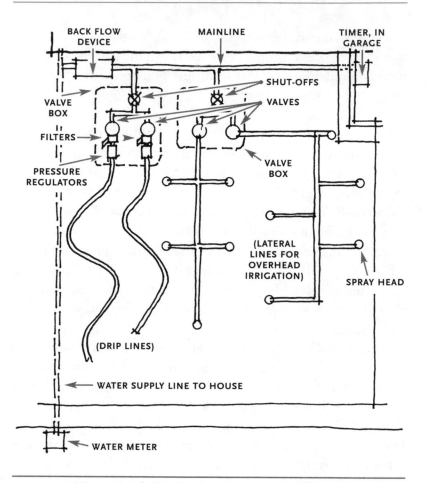

Relationships among valves, mainline, and laterals

your water take-off point, you'll need a separate little trench to the timer from the mainline at some point.

You are now ready for some "real" work.

INSTALLATION—THINKING BEYOND "CUT AND GLUE"

Okay, my brawny brethren, it's your turn now. We still need that brain, though, so don't check it in just yet. To make all this come together, we need *all* of you.

Trenching

Yes, it's time to trench. There are easy and hard ways to trench. I'll let you discover all the hard ways on your own. The easy way is to aquaficate.

"Aquafication" is the technical term (okay, you won't find it in any other book) for presoaking your trenches. The technique is as follows. Make one pass with a shovel or pick along *all* your lines. Allow yourself one short panting spell, then clean the dirt out and fill the trenches with water. Retire for the rest of the day with a nice cool drink. The next morning, your trenches will practically dig themselves.

An alternative to aquafication is renting a trencher. This fine machine has saved many a back. Trenchers work best in large yards with long runs, since they are big, unwieldy, and difficult to maneuver. I don't normally use a trencher in most average-sized yards unless the soil is just terribly compacted or rocky. And in really large yards, I'll rent the riding kind. (The walk-behind types are difficult for any operator less beefy than King Kong to control.)

You need to dig your mainline trench at least eighteen inches deep to protect the pipe from future changes of grade or from inadvertent excavation. (Lateral lines, which you'll dig later, can be only a foot deep). Remember that the existence of any one shallow spot will raise your pipe up to that level over a long distance, so follow the weakest-link principle in your digging (see illustration on next page).

Verify (so that you can avoid) the locations of any and all underground utilities before trenching, *especially* if you use power equipment. Please, learn from my mistakes, not your own. The first time I broke a water line—and, no, it was not the last—was on a Friday night. My clients wanted to shower before going out to dinner, and I was so distressed I actually broke down and sobbed when I couldn't get a plumber out till the next day. At least if you hit your own water line, I suppose, you have no one but yourself to blame.

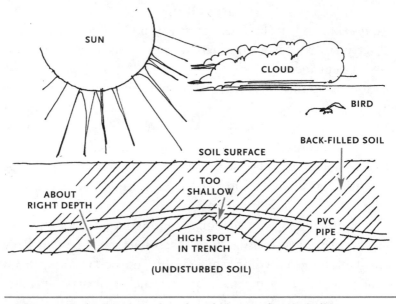

One high spot makes the whole trench too shallow.

Underground Service Alert (see "Sources" at the end of the book) will mark many but not all utilities if you call them several days before you dig. But only *you* know or can find out the location of your leach lines, or where you ran electricity out to the shed or the propane line to the heater. U.S.A. only verifies *public* utilities, and often only as far as the meter that they serve.

Installing the Mainline

It's best to install and test the mainline before you tackle the laterals. I'm not going to talk much about the cutting, gluing, and fitting aspects of irrigation installation, since if you can read this book then you can read the directions on the back of

EXTREMELY IMPORTANT QUICK TIP
Don't buy cheap irrigation parts. Get all your stuff at an irrigation supply place, not the corner hardware or some big-box store. Oh, have I mentioned this before? The ten dollars you save on a rinky-dink valve will be long forgotten if it ever malfunctions while you're on vacation.

the can of glue (or ask the guy in the store). Instead I'll share some of the little tricks no one else will ever tell you.

Begin your mainline installation by turning off your water upstream of your water take-off point. Then you can connect your irrigation to the water supply by unscrewing a faucet (you can reinstall it after replacing it with a T fitting) or cutting into your water line (much trickier). Or, if you are very lucky, a clairvoyant plumber will have anticipated your need and provided you with a "stub-out" for this very purpose.

Only You Can Prevent "Backflow"

Install a backflow prevention device downstream from your water take-off point. A backflow device protects the water supply from contamination that could occur if there is a drop in pressure, causing dirty or—heaven forbid—pesticide-laden water to be sucked back from your yard and into the water supply. (Most communities require them, though I have never heard of a homeowner getting dinged for not installing one.) Once your backflow device is installed, it can act as the shut-off for your entire irrigation installation, so you can now turn your water back on.

Many homeowners (and some contractors) will install anti-siphon valves instead of using a backflow device in conjunction with inline valves. Anti-siphon valves must be installed six inches higher than the highest head they serve in order to function properly. This could mean valves six feet above ground level if your manifold is at the bottom of a hill and your heads run along the top! Of course, most installers don't read the fine print and neglect to do this, rendering the valves useless for the purpose for which they were intended. Let me just tell you that anti-siphon valves are a cheap, cheesy way to go, and leave it at that. The only time I use them is if I am installing only one or two valves, if the homeowner is on a tight budget, or if I'm adding onto an existing system that already has them.

Avoiding Mainline Misery

All the pipe for your mainline should be thick-walled "schedule 40" so that when you do hit it with a shovel— and you will—it won't snap like an eggshell. Pipe is cheap, so don't skimp on it. Especially on a mainline.

If you live in an area where freezing is a possibility, any components of your irrigation system that are always under pressure and are above ground need to be protected. (This is yet another reason for your mainline to be buried at least eighteen inches deep—the earth is a great insulator.) Wrap your exposed pipes with insulating tape, and if your backflow device is above ground, buy one of those incredibly expensive blankets (a "frost bag") for it. Or build it a nice, warm, insulated house, if you prefer.

Sizing It Up

The size of your backflow device, pipe, and valves will depend on the gpm available to you. Be aware that you will lose flow (gpm) over long distances due to pressure loss from the friction of the water in your pipe. I bump up the size of pipe I would normally use by one size for runs of between, say, fifty and a hundred feet. (And if your mainline is over a hundred feet, I'll bet you should be using the services of a professional designer, so I won't even go there.)

If you have less than 8 gpm available, three-quarter-inch materials are just fine. Between 8 and 13 gpm, I'll use one-inch pipe and components. Between 13 and 20 gpm, I'll go up to inch-and-a-quarter pipe with an inch-and-a-half-backflow and valves. With really big yards and higher gpms, the intricacies of pipe sizing for the mainline and laterals can be more than you *or* I would want to tackle. For example, you may end up needing an inch-and-a-half mainline

QUICK TIP
Overdesign your irrigation and you will be a happy, happy person. Underdesign it and you will be sour and peevish the rest of your natural life.

and inch-and-a-half, one-inch, and three-quarter-inch valves, all serving lateral lines with different pipe sizes . . . If you are dealing with that level of complexity you really should get experienced, certified and/or licensed, professional help.

Fun with Valves

Unless you use anti-siphon valves, you will be installing your valves below ground, in those green boxes you always wondered about. Dig the valve box holes much bigger than you think you need to; it's always good to have room to maneuver. If you have more than a couple of valve manifolds, it is a good idea to supply each with its own shut-off valve so that you don't have to shut down the whole system if there is a problem with just one valve. And if you have gophers, line that box with aviary wire or hardware cloth, or they'll have those valves buried in dirt before you can put the lid back on.

QUICK TIP
Use more Teflon tape than they tell you to! I wrap it round and round till the threads are a blur, and my threaded fittings never leak.

Make sure you install your valves far enough apart so that you could unscrew one, if you had to. Otherwise, when you return from your holiday and have to replace that cheap valve you bought against my better advice, you'll have to tear apart and redo the entire manifold, and that is really a pain once all your lateral lines are hooked up to those valves.

ANOTHER QUICK TIP
Flush out your mainline thoroughly before installing your valves. If you get a pebble stuck in the diaphragm of your valve, you will have to take the whole thing apart to get it out. Big pain.

Getting Wired

Now go ahead and wire up your valves to your timer, following the instructions that come with it. Multistrand 18-gauge wire is fine for most applications, but for very long distances switch to single-strand 14-gauge wire. Tape the wires to the underside of your mainline where they'll be protected, and always run an extra wire or two in case one malfunctions later. On big jobs, especially in gopher country, I'll run one extra wire to each manifold, since it is so difficult to run new wires over vast, already landscaped areas, and since wire, like pipe, is cheap.

Begin by wiring one of the two wires from each valve's solenoid to the white, "common" wire. With three or fewer valves, you may be able to wire all three wires to the common wire in one connection—if not, or if you have more than three valves, you can piggyback two at a time. Once all valves have been connected to the common wire, connect each of the remaining wires on each solenoid to a different colored (if multistrand) or numbered (by you, if single strand) wire. Then, wire the corresponding wires to the timer (one white common and a different colored or numbered wire for each valve).

Do use gel cap wire connectors, not just electrical tape, since your connections will be below ground and subjected to moisture. And do be careful not to inadvertently nick or strip the insulation from your wiring, causing a short.

Testing, One, Two . . .

Once all the components of your system are installed, you'll want to test it to make sure everything works as it should before tackling your lateral lines. The first step is to run a pressure test. Because the mainline, like the plumbing in your house, is always under pressure, it is important that it be well glued and threaded so that there are no leaks. Make sure the valves are turned off, and then turn on the backflow device (or other shutoff if you opted not to install a backflow). If there are no immediate and obvious problems—twenty-foot geysers, etc.—

QUICK TIP

Wire up your valves to your timer completely before plugging it in. Why? Because otherwise you'll blow its little brains out. I don't know why this happens, or why there isn't a warning in one-inch-high bright-red letters in the directions. I've blown up two or three timers in my time. And good-quality ones are *expensive*.

check for moisture underneath each threaded fitting. If you discover a tiny bead of water beneath a threaded joint, do not despair. Nine times out of ten, it'll seal up by the next day. Glued fittings are another matter. Redo them.

Now test your timer. If one valve doesn't work, the problem is probably in the connections or wiring to that one valve. If none of the valves work, you probably have a problem with the common wire.

Installing the Lateral Lines

Once the mainline is in and functioning, you can install your lateral lines, both drip and spray. Start with your overhead spray lines, though, since even the most perfectly designed spray pattern will overlap onto non-target areas. Thus, a plant you may have intended to drip irrigate may already receive water from a nearby lawn's spray heads.

Lay out each line so that pipe use and trenching are minimized, and so the valve is more or less centered in the line (reducing cumulative friction loss to the far heads). And mark out all your lines at once, because in many cases pipes from two dif-

QUICK TIP

After you've trenched, assemble one line at a time so that you don't accidentally put a head from one line onto the pipe for another. Using color-coded flags to mark the heads of different lines makes this much easier.

ferent valves will share a trench. (In that case, make sure the trench is wide enough to allow the pipes to lie side by side. If they are stacked one on top of the other, and years

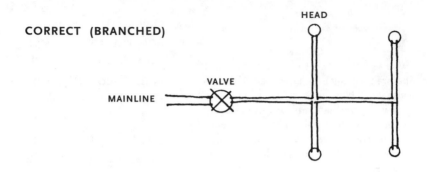

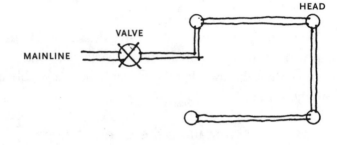

Lateral line pipe layout

from now you have to fix a break in the bottom one . . . well, you won't be happy. Always make sure to leave at least an inch and a half of space between two pipes.)

You can either use schedule 40 pipe again, or downgrade to "class 200" pipe, which is lighter and cheaper. Do be aware that schedule 40 pipe, though stronger, will reduce your available gpm, because its thicker wall creates a smaller interior diameter.

Pipe Sizing for Lateral Lines

When using three-quarter-inch valves, I use three-quarter-inch pipe and fittings throughout. I don't know any professionals who bother with half-inch materials. But when I use one-inch or inch-and-a-half valves, I downsize my pipe and fittings as I go downstream along the line. The idea is that a pipe near the valve that must supply perhaps five heads downstream at 3 gpm each (for a total of 15 gpm running through it) needs to be

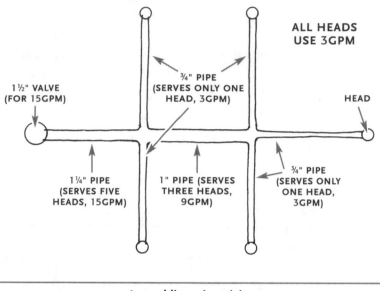

ALL HEADS
USE 3GPM

1½" VALVE
(FOR 15GPM)

¾" PIPE
(SERVES ONLY ONE
HEAD, 3GPM)

HEAD

1¼" PIPE
(SERVES FIVE
HEADS, 15GPM)

1" PIPE (SERVES
THREE HEADS,
9GPM)

¾" PIPE
(SERVES ONLY
ONE HEAD,
3GPM)

Lateral line pipe sizing

larger than one toward the end of the line that supplies only one head (and 3 gpm).

Reducing your pipe size also increases the pressure toward the end of the line, where it tends to be lower due to friction loss. You can use the same gpm-to-pipe-size relationships that you used to calculate your mainline size, though in fact class 200 pipe permits greater flow than schedule 40. In any case, in most city lots fine-tuning your pipe sizing is more a nicety than a necessity, and is best left to those with too much time (or gpm) on their hands . . .

More Testing

Once you have hooked up your first lateral line, you should test it before moving on to the others. Why? Because with all those charts and specifications for psi, gpm, nozzles full, half, and quarter, and sprays strip, flat, and low, chances are you may have made at least one mistake. One that may blow all your carefully laid out plans right out of the water.

Turn on the valve to thoroughly flush out all the dirt in the line before attaching any of the heads. If you have several children, you can have one at each head location except the last, plugging the risers with their tiny thumbs. If you are solo, you can cheat a little by screwing on the heads closest to the valve first and working your way toward the last one.

Once your heads are all threaded onto the risers, turn on the valve again. If you have made a major blunder, you'll know it right away. But even if you think you've done yourself proud, go ahead and adjust each head to cover the space allotted to it, and make sure that the water from one head reaches all the way to the next one. Let the station run for three or four minutes so you can be certain that all areas are truly getting wet and that there are no missed spots. Believe me, you'll find those spots soon enough once your yard has been planted and green turns to brown. And it is such a pain to add or move valves or heads once the sod is laid, the plants planted, and the mulch mulching. So cast a critical eye about before breaking out the champagne.

> **QUICK TIP**
>
> It is almost always a good idea to install your heads on "swing joints" so that when someone drives onto, walks into, or otherwise abuses a sprinkler head, it doesn't break the underground fitting it screws into. Broken heads or the risers that support them are no big deal; broken pipes and fittings, on the other hand, will bring out the worst in you. And you can almost entirely avoid them by using flexible risers or swing joints. (Ask your irrigation place to show you how they work.)

Before You Backfill . . .

When you have finished flushing and checking all your overhead lateral lines, you may fill the trenches back in. First make sure you don't need those trenches for anything else, though. Take a moment. Think you'll ever want electrical in the back forty? Run some conduit now, just in case. Thinking of putting in lighting? A good route to run cable might coincide with one of your lines.

If your heads are more than eight inches or so above grade (perhaps to shoot over the tops of plantings), you should stake the risers. I use hose clamps to attach them to pieces of rebar pounded next to—not through!—the lateral line. Don't set the grade of your lawn heads yet, though—wait till just before you seed or lay your sod, when you have completed your final grading and leveling.

Ahhh, it's so much easier to backfill than to trench, isn't it? Just make sure you still have that space between any two pipes sharing a trench, and also that you don't shovel big stones directly on top of a pipe (where they can crack it if driven on). And while you're at it, flood the trenches when they are about two-thirds full of soil, to help compact them to the same level as previously. This is especially important in lawn areas, where a poorly compacted trench will show up as a sunken line.

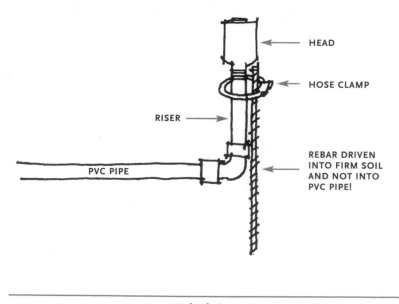

Staked riser

Installing Drip Lines

Even if you hire a professional to install your mainline and spray laterals, you will almost certainly want to install your own lateral drip lines (the part downstream from the valve). First, because drip lines are so easy to put in. Second, because, since they are installed after planting, they don't fit the scheduling for the rest of your irrigation. Besides, you're the one who will be maintaining, expanding, and repairing them over the years, so you should become familiar with how they work.

Filters and Pressure Regulators

You will of course install a pressure regulator and a filter (get the more expensive, flushable Y filter) before you attach the drip tubing to the valve. You may be able to get away with a single filter installed upstream of all your drip valves, but if you have

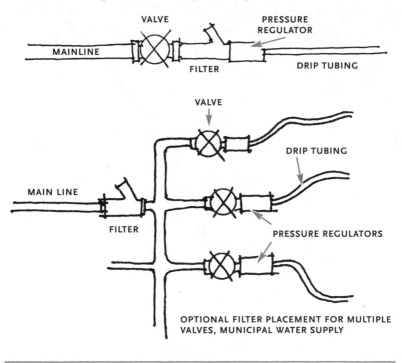

Drip valve, filter, pressure regulator

dirty water you are better off installing one directly after each valve, to decrease the total load on each filter. Make sure the filters are readily accessible, particularly if you are on a well and may have lots of particulate matter in your water. I know some people who have to flush their filters after each cycle of watering. (But they really should talk to their well-and-pump guy about an automatic back-flushing sand filter.)

You should put in a separate 20- or 25-psi pressure regulator downstream of each valve and any filter (so that both valve and filter operate at full pressure). If you neglect to reduce the pressure for your drip line, your fittings will blow apart. Maybe not immediately, but they will, they will. And you'll be none the wiser till you discover the gullies raging through the perennial bed, the mudflow across the driveway.

Getting Tubular

Now you can attach your tubing, but first run your overhead irrigation so you know what areas don't need to be drip irrigated. If you're not sure if a given area gets enough water or not, run tubing there anyway in case it turns out you need to add emitters onto it later.

Contrary to what you might think, drip should be laid on *top* of the ground (and then covered by mulch) so that the tubing is easier to find and fix later, and because emitters get clogged too easily if they're in direct contact with dirt. The only exceptions are when your line must cross a long unplanted distance or go under a pathway. You can switch to buried PVC pipe in such areas, reverting to tubing again when needed.

Because the quarter-inch "spaghetti" line often used to extend an emitter is so flimsy and easily displaced, you should lay out your primary half-inch tubing as close to your plants as possible without kinking it. This will also save you time, since simply adding a branch to your half-inch line can often eliminate long multiple runs of spaghetti tubing.

Always lay all your half-inch tubing for a given line before

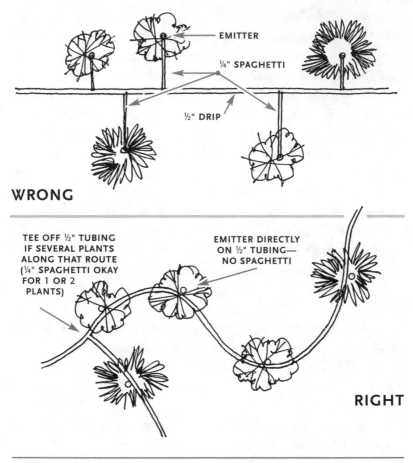

Drip line laterals in planting beds

you begin putting on the emitters, or you can accidentally put an emitter on the wrong drip line. Use lots and lots of U-shaped "jute staples" (used for jute netting) to hold the tubing down, and mark the ends of the lines so you can find them later. (Part of routine drip system maintenance is the periodic flushing of your tubing.)

Once your tubing is laid, you need to run water through it to get all the dirt out. Starting closest to the valve, close off all your ends except the furthest and turn on the valve. Then close that end and open the next furthest till your lines are clean,

clean, clean. You don't *ever* want to put *any* emitters into tubing with even a *chance* of dirt in it. Clogging is the number one cause of long-term drip system failures. You should keep your tubing cleaner than you do your own mouth.

Strategic Emitter Placement

Place your emitter(s) between the edge of the root ball and the center of the plant. If the emitter is too close to the crown of the plant, it can cause crown rot; if it is too far out, it simply won't water the root ball. I have seen a totally dry (and dead) plant surrounded by wet soil when the emitter was installed next to—but not quite on—the root ball of the plant.

A four-inch pot or a one-gallon sized plant are usually fine with a single emitter to start with, but use at least two emitters

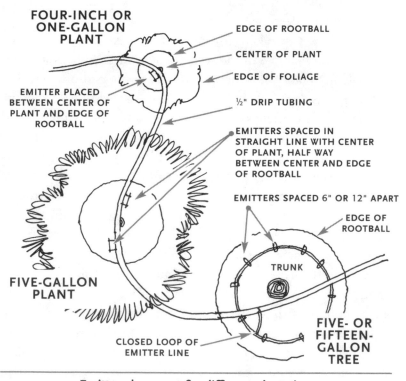

FOUR-INCH OR
ONE-GALLON
PLANT

EDGE OF ROOTBALL

CENTER OF PLANT

EDGE OF FOLIAGE

EMITTER PLACED
BETWEEN CENTER OF
PLANT AND EDGE OF
ROOTBALL

½" DRIP TUBING

EMITTERS SPACED IN
STRAIGHT LINE WITH CENTER
OF PLANT, HALF WAY
BETWEEN CENTER AND EDGE
OF ROOTBALL

EMITTERS SPACED 6" OR 12" APART

EDGE OF
ROOTBALL

TRUNK

FIVE-GALLON
PLANT

FIVE- OR
FIFTEEN-
GALLON
TREE

CLOSED LOOP OF
EMITTER LINE

Emitter placement for different plant sizes

for five-gallon plants, placing them at opposite sides of the root ball so that the whole mass is moistened. With larger plants and trees, I like to use "emitter line," which is like spaghetti tubing with emitters already in it. Not only does this save a lot of tedious fabrication of emitter necklaces around large root balls, but emitter line is less prone to clogging than plain emitters are.

Testing and Troubleshooting

When you finish your drip line, turn it on and see how it works. If there is no water flow, or greatly reduced water flow, at the end of the line, it can be one of three things: a kink in the tubing, a blowout you haven't found yet, or too many emitters / too long a run of pipe for the given line. Correct this, and then double- and triple-check that you didn't forget to provide emitters to any plants. I just hate finding those poor babies later, droopy or even dead . . .

Check the system again throughout the next couple of weeks, and then every couple of months or so, to make sure you didn't leave off any plants, that no emitters have popped off, and that no tubing has come apart. You may also want to add or remove emitters to plants near overhead irrigation lines, as mentioned earlier. Young plants are not very forgiving of lapses in watering, so be especially vigilant till they're established—maybe three months or so after planting.

The proof of any irrigation system comes in the months or even years after its installation. I figure that at least ninety percent of the callbacks I get are irrigation related. Usually, the culprit is an overzealous client, drowning the very investment she strives to protect. But sometimes I find the emitterless plant, the poorly adjusted nozzle or misplaced head. You should figure on finding these things, too, and doing some fine-tuning in the weeks and months after installation. But, most important, you'll need to learn the needs of your particular garden, and set your timer to respond to them throughout the seasons. Then, and only then, are you done with your irrigation.

 Chapter 7

Planting

The Fun Part

Finally, it is time to plant. You've trenched and you've shoveled, you've heaved and you've hauled, and perhaps you've even hurled (epithets, anyway). But look around at what all you've accomplished. And now, the really fun part begins.

HOW (AND WHEN) TO BUY PLANTS

The way to buy plants is all at once, from your lists, right before you are ready to put them in the ground. The reason to buy them all at once is so you can set them out in one go, moving and rearranging them as needed to tweak your plan. You will be setting out and then planting your plants in a specific order (which I'll describe in the next section of this chapter, "Layout"). Another reason to buy all your plants at once, from one place (as I mentioned in Chapter 1), is to be able to angle for a discount.

Use your landscape plan to compile a list of the plants you'll need so that you avoid buying on impulse, succumbing to the charms of whatever happens to be blooming at the nursery that week. A month or so before you think you'll be ready to plant, give this list to a couple of different nurseries. They may have some plants in stock, and others they can order. Ask them to bid on the entire order, including delivery, if needed. Ask them what kind of a break they will give you if you get the whole lot from them. This arrangement works well for both you and the nursery. You don't waste time running around to different places, and you save money, which is always fun; they don't waste time selling you the plants.

You will probably discover that some of the plants you want simply aren't available from any source, in which case you'll need to make substitutions. If you did your own design, ask the nurseryman or woman for a recommendation, since he or she will know comparable, obtainable plants. If you used a designer, ask her where to get the plants she specified, or to give you alternative choices.

Try to arrange for delivery right before you plant. The nursery is very good at keeping container plants alive. You probably are not, and every day you have custody of your plants is another day you could forget to water them. Overgrown plants can croak in a single day if you underwater them, and certain drought-lovers will yellow at a drop too much. The longer the plants hang around at your house, the worse they'll look and the more stressed they'll be when you finally plant them.

Plants to Avoid

There are two instances in which you should reject plants. Avoid plants with poorly developed root systems, indicating that the plant was only recently moved up from a smaller container. (Such plants will often look suspiciously small for their container size.) You should be able to upend the can without all the dirt falling out; the roots should form a cohesive root ball. If you must accept a poorly rooted plant (perhaps it is the only *Fagus sylvatica* 'Tricolor' to be had in your county), be very careful when planting it so that the newly forming roots aren't destroyed when you remove the plant from the can. Above all, do not pull the plant out, but rather, turn that can upside down into your waiting cupped hand.

The other kind of plant to avoid is the one that has been in the can too long. Although this fault can be harder to spot, it is much more common. In this case, the plant is often exceptionally *large* for the container it's sold in, thrilling the unwary buyer. (Or it will show signs of having been heavily pruned, indicating that it was once too large.) Such plants are called "root-bound," and will have big, thick, circling roots all around the outside of the root ball. In extreme cases roots will show up on the surface of the soil in the can, or even sprout through the drainage holes, as well. In fact, I've seen fifteen-foot-tall trees growing from one-gallon cans. But just try and take one home—any tree that big has sunk roots deep into the soil, believe me. It may *look* like it's still in a can, but don't be fooled—it's already "planted."

The problem with overgrown plants is that the roots can become a container of their own, strangling the plant and preventing its roots from ever growing properly into the surrounding soil once it is properly planted. If you do purchase such a plant (and it can be worth it for a hard-to-find prize), then make sure that you perform radical surgery on those roots before you set it into the ground. (see the section "Planting 101," on page 175).

You will notice that I've barely mentioned the part of the plant you can actually see. That is because, with the exception of trees (which I'll discuss separately, toward the end of this chapter), what you are really buying is a root system. The problem with selecting plants on the basis of their top growth is that, for many plants, the top growth is relatively impermanent. Think about it. Perennials and grasses are cut to the ground every winter. Deciduous plants lose all their leaves. And even some broadleaf evergreens benefit from the occasional renewal pruning. Almost any poorly shaped plant can be worked over via judicious thinning and heading. But the roots—if they are a disaster, the plant is doomed.

Another myth I'd like to debunk is that of the "sick" plant. A couple of curled leaves, a scorched bit here and there, a stray aphid—these are not life-threatening conditions! If you have a pimple, or a hangover, or blisters, say, are you unfit for service?

We have such unnaturally high expectations of health and beauty (look at what we've done to fruit in this country!) that we forget it's natural and normal, and not a bit unhealthy, to have a few dings and bruises to show for the life we've lived.

In general, nursery stock looks its best in the spring, will start to get a bit shopworn by fall, and can look downright ratty by winter. But that doesn't mean that it won't be just fine once you get it in the ground. Most plants that look bad at the nursery just need to be planted. Smart gardeners know this, and can sometimes pick up bargains that more finicky buyers would pass up.

There are a few instances in which a plant really *is* sick, or harbors a pest problem that could get out of hand, but chances are you wouldn't necessarily know what to look for. Your best bet is to deal with a reputable nursery and let them be the ones to decide whether to sell you a plant or not. Because almost every retail nursery stands behind its stock (even when a buyer's negligence or ignorance is to blame for its demise), it has a vested interest in a plant's warrantability.

LAYOUT: THE VISION TAKES SHAPE

Before you begin laying out your plants, double-check to make sure your grading is everything it should be, since once plants are in the ground it will be too late to correct the odd low spot. Then begin by placing your trees. I always set out the biggest and most important trees first, then the smaller, less critical ones. Check the placement from different vantage points throughout the property. Will this tree shade the patio? Will that one be too close to the sidewalk? Will the far one block the view of the surrounding hills?

You'll find that the best design in the world will still need your creative interpretation, and the worst will need a sound thrashing. Don't be afraid to tweak and adjust your plan to fit the reality of your site. It is not the drawing on paper but the resulting garden that is important. Double-check the projected size of the plants at maturity, particularly their width, so that you avoid overcrowding (or underplanting) and can head off future maintenance hassles caused by plants being too close to walkways and buildings.

Once all your trees are in the right spots, plant them (see the section "Trees," below). Then lay out your large evergreen shrubs. I always begin with these because they will form the underlying structure revealed so plainly in the winter. Make sure they carry out your design intent, whatever it was—to screen objectionable views, or to provide a sense of substance or enclosure, for example. And double-check that their spacing correlates with their projected width. Dense plantings do provide less space for opportunistic weeds, but if it turns out, for example, that you are trying to squeeze three photinias into a four-foot spot (it looked bigger on paper), then it is time to rethink your plan.

Next lay out your large deciduous shrubs and vines, then your smaller plants, first evergreen and then deciduous. Finally, you can lay out your groundcovers and perennials. Since these are considered filler plants, their placement is least crucial to the success of your planting plan.

Because you will probably be buying plants that ultimately get big in larger-sized containers to start with, another way to lay out your plants is by container size. And if you don't think you can get them all planted in a couple of days, you should plant each type or size directly after laying them out, so that you don't have plants sitting out in the hot sun for long periods of time, neglected, unloved, and almost certainly wilting.

PLANTING 101

Ah, the atrocities I've witnessed in the name of planting. I've seen plants buried so deeply that only a few tufts of green remained above soil level. I've rescued "planted" plants still in their cans. And then there was the guy, owner of Fly-By-Nite Landscaping, who suggested I just hack the roots off my plants so I wouldn't have to dig such big holes for them. Oh, sure, fella. Where did *you* get *your* degree?

Enough of the *don't's* of planting. How about some *do's*? Do dig a hole somewhat wider but not much deeper than the root ball. If the ground is hard, start the hole and fill it with water, then come back in a few hours to finish it. (And if water is still standing there, you have a drainage problem. For help, go directly to "Soil Types" and "Drainage Woes" in Chapter 5.)

The reason you don't want an enormous hole, contrary to popular thinking, is not just to avoid the hard labor of digging it. The reason is that at some point the plant's roots must come into contact with, and adapt to, your real soil. The sooner this happens, the better. The goal when planting is not to create a new, larger container of perfect soil (and this is only feasible with small plants in any case), but to ease the transition to your real dirt. Another reason not to dig too deep a hole is that you don't want to place a plant on freshly dug soil, because it will later compact, causing the plant to sink too low in relation to the surrounding grade.

Upend the plant can, thumping and squeezing it if necessary, until the plant is free of its plastic home. (Pulling a plant out by its top is the last resort. The *second*-to-last resort is cutting the can open.) Examine the roots. If the plant is barely rooted and soil is collapsing all around, tenderly place the plant as best you can in the hole right away. If the soil holds together, and you can see a few roots around the edge where the can was, rough them up a bit and place the plant in the hole. If what you see are roots

> **QUICK TIP**
>
> Even if the roots look fine and don't need cutting, it's a good idea to cut back any plants which seem overly large for the size container they're in. Big-headed plants dry out more quickly both in the can and out, and tend to be more stressed by planting than smaller ones. It's simply too much for a root system that has just been disturbed by the act of planting to have to support such a large top. Cut the plant back to a "normal" size for the container it's in.

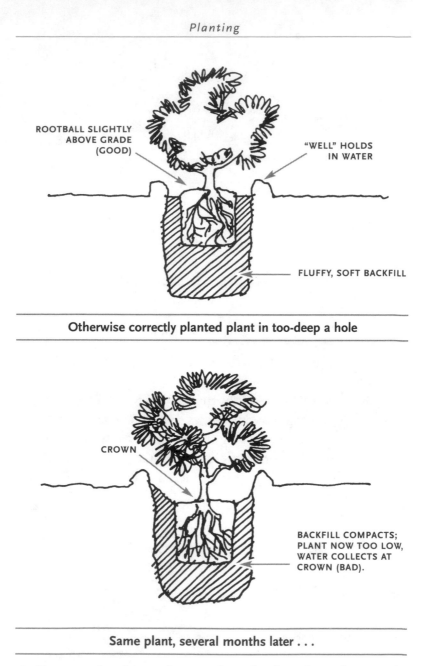

ROOTBALL SLIGHTLY
ABOVE GRADE
(GOOD)

"WELL" HOLDS
IN WATER

FLUFFY, SOFT BACKFILL

Otherwise correctly planted plant in too-deep a hole

CROWN

BACKFILL COMPACTS;
PLANT NOW TOO LOW,
WATER COLLECTS AT
CROWN (BAD).

Same plant, several months later . . .

circling round and round, get a sharp knife and cut them so the
plant knows it is out of the can: I usually score the sides of the
root ball from top to bottom in three or four places and then
make a big X across the bottom. If you cut a lot of roots and the

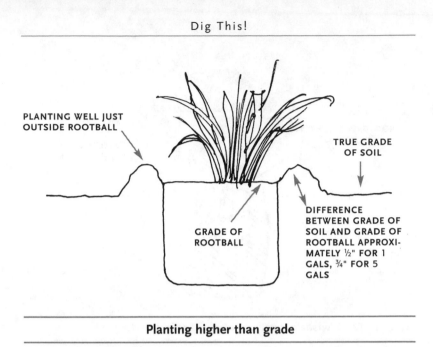

PLANTING WELL JUST
OUTSIDE ROOTBALL

TRUE GRADE
OF SOIL

GRADE OF
ROOTBALL

DIFFERENCE
BETWEEN GRADE OF
SOIL AND GRADE OF
ROOTBALL APPROXI-
MATELY ½" FOR 1
GALS, ¾" FOR 5
GALS

Planting higher than grade

plant has a big top, compensate by pruning back some of that
top growth.

If you amended your soil throughout, or if you are planting in
topsoil, you can begin backfilling as soon as you have made sure
the plant is at the correct height in relation to the surrounding
grade. What is the correct height? Higher, that's what. Plants
don't need to be a lot higher than the surrounding soil—about a

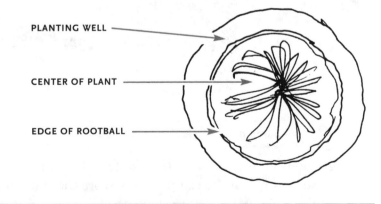

PLANTING WELL

CENTER OF PLANT

EDGE OF ROOTBALL

Planting well (top view)

half-inch higher for one gallons, and maybe three-quarters of an inch for fives—but if you plant them at grade they will sink over time, and water will be trapped at the crown, which is ultrasensitive to excess moisture. So plant high.

If you are planting in unamended soil, it's a good idea to mix a little organic matter into your backfill. A couple of shovelfuls of compost for a five-gallon, and less for a one-gallon, is plenty unless you really have problem soil (then you need more). I also incorporate a slow-release fertilizer into the backfill, unless it was already added during the soil preparation.

QUICK TIP

With large plants (five gallons or more) it's not a bad idea to water once when the hole is half backfilled, and again when you've built your well. This increases the chance that water will penetrate all the way to the bottom of the hole (and the root ball).

Make an earthen berm just outside the root ball to create a little well that will hold the water in around your freshly planted plant. Water it. Then water it again, and yet again. Not sure if you're watering enough? Unplant a plant you've just watered. If the soil isn't wet at the bottom of the hole, you still haven't watered it enough. You need to thoroughly soak the dirt around a newly planted plant in order to eliminate air bubbles and settle the soil.

Though it isn't necessary to water each plant the minute it goes in, don't let plants sit unwatered more than an hour or two, especially if the weather is warm. In fact, if the day is really a scorcher, just hold off on planting altogether till it cools off.

WHY PLANTS DIE

The best way to ensure successful planting is to understand why and how plants die. A newly planted plant is a vulnerable, traumatized creature. Plucked from the plastic can in which it has spent its entire life, its manhandled roots must now cope with real soil, no matter how generously amended. Previously protected from extremes of heat and cold by shade cloth or the close proximity of other plants, the plant now finds itself exposed to the elements as well as the predations of dog and child, snail and gopher.

Ninety-nine point nine nine percent of plants that die do so from water-related causes. Initially, they die from a lack of water. Later, they'll die from an excess of the same element. "How can this be?" you may well ask.

Let's examine thirst-related mortality. How can you, well-intentioned and anxious new plant parent that you are, ease what is called "transplant stress"? First of all, never plant a dry plant. Be sure to keep your charges moist in the interval between their arrival and their placement in the soil. Second, don't let your plants sit too long after planting without that long, deep drink of water. Third, keep them moist in the crucial first two weeks or so after planting, when they are most susceptible to shock. It is almost impossible to overwater new plantings.

Which leads us nicely to the fact that it is very easy to overwater plants *after* they're established. In fact, if you have a very heavy clay soil, it can be darn near impossible *not* to overwater. Remember how in Chapter 5 I discussed the drainage characteristics of the different soil types? If you have heavy soil, your drainage must be perfect and the timing of your irrigation faultless in order to minimize plant deaths of all but the most cast-iron species.

Overwatering is much more serious than underwatering, though its initial symptoms appear more benign. While underwatered plants look like hell—at first droopy and limp, and later scorched and burnt—even the most awful looking victims will usually recover, given enough time. (Unfortunately, many people assume such plants are "dead," and stop watering them. Though the leaves may be goners, if the stems and branches are still green underneath the bark, chances are the plant will recover and produce nice, green new growth.)

Overwatering causes the roots and/or the crown (the point at which the roots meet the shoots) of a plant to rot. Early indicators are yellow leaves, especially in the interior or lower portions of a plant. The anxious neophyte gardener will often respond to this cry for help with more water, thus sealing the fate of a plant that was already in deep trouble.

The first thing to do when you see yellow leaves is to check the moisture of the soil at the original root ball. If it is moist, make sure that it dries out to a depth of at least an inch before the next irrigation cycle is due to come on, and re-program your clock accordingly. The problem is, roots that rot don't rejuvenate quickly—or at all, in some cases.

SPECIAL NEEDS PLANTS

Some plants just march—or grow, I guess—to a different drummer. Clematis, for example, demands that its roots be kept cool (mulch extra thickly, or shade them with other plants in close proximity). Daphnes sulk and die if their roots are so much as nicked in planting. And certain riparian plants actually love to be planted too low. But rather than list each plant according to its whims, I'll just focus on two types that need special attention: trees, and plants purchased bare root or balled and burlapped (called "b and b").

Trees

There are a few things you should know about trees. First, a tree's form as a young specimen can predict its viability and structural strength at maturity. Second, the damage done to this form by poor staking or pruning is usually irreversible. What should you look for when buying trees? The operative word is "balance." The top should be in balance with the trunk and roots, and the branches on one side should balance those on the other.

Bigger is not necessarily better, particularly when you are judging the canopy of a tree. A big-headed tree is often a root-bound tree. Exceptionally full trees can also have problems supporting themselves if their trunks are not commensurately stout. In addition, fat-headed "lollipop" trees are more likely to lose those heads, so to speak, in a high wind. Dense foliage acts like a sail, catching the breeze instead of allowing it to pass through the tree.

Bigger *is* better when it comes to the trunk, however. The caliper (thickness) of a young tree's trunk is a good indicator of its strength. In fact, the price of many boxed trees is based on their caliper, rather than height or width. Trunks should also taper so

QUICK TIP
When transporting trees, know that they are just fine lying down in the bed of your pickup. If you place them upright, the sixty-mile-an-hour-plus winds of the freeway will either blow them over or snap their poor leafy heads off . . .

that they are thicker at the bottom than at the top. Lack of caliper and taper can both be traced back to poor practices by growers, who tend to stake trees too tightly and grow them too quickly. But it's hard to blame the growers. Since it can take years for them to produce their product, whoever can respond to the fluctuations of the marketplace the most quickly wins.

Reject any tree with a forked leader (the "leader" is the central stem of a tree's canopy—the continuation of the trunk, if you will). Such a tree is unsound, since the juncture of the two "tines" is almost always narrow and

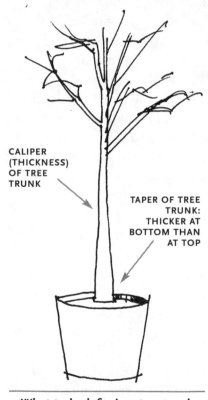

CALIPER (THICKNESS) OF TREE TRUNK

TAPER OF TREE TRUNK: THICKER AT BOTTOM THAN AT TOP

What to look for in a tree trunk

subject to splitting. (This is a problem only with species inclined toward a single leader. Multitrunked specimens, such as many Japanese maples or crape myrtles, can have forked (multiple) leaders without any problems.)

Most important of all, with any tree, check for any large wounds along the trunk. Particularly inauspicious is any break in the bark that threatens to circle the trunk, rather than going lengthwise along it. Such a cut can girdle (strangle) the tree, cutting off the passage of food and water from roots to top.

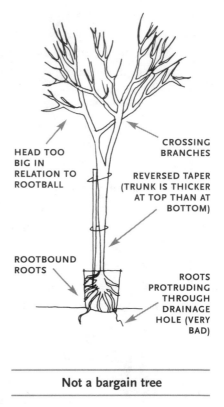

HEAD TOO BIG IN RELATION TO ROOTBALL

CROSSING BRANCHES

REVERSED TAPER (TRUNK IS THICKER AT TOP THAN AT BOTTOM)

ROOTBOUND ROOTS

ROOTS PROTRUDING THROUGH DRAINAGE HOLE (VERY BAD)

Not a bargain tree

Avoid trees with a lot of crossing branches, or those with branches that originate at too narrow an angle to the trunk (these tend to split off at maturity). Though such defects, like full-headedness, can often be corrected by pruning, the skills required fill volumes. Also avoid trees with many more branches on one side than on the other. While you can always thin out excess

QUICK TIP

To ensure that your hole is not too deep, and that the tree will be planted at the correct height before you lower it into the ground, measure the depth of the soil in the container and check it against the depth of the hole (place a stick across the hole and measure down from it). With boxed trees, this is essential, because once a large tree is down in a deep hole, it can be nearly impossible to lift it out again in order to raise its level.

branches, it can take years for a bald side to fill in.

In planting trees, it is extra critical that they be planted high, and that the hole be dug not much deeper than the root ball, because trees are even more susceptible to crown rot than most plants, and because your investment in them is so much greater.

Staking

Any tree capable of supporting its own trunk should *not* be staked. But if the tree wants to bend way over when you remove the stake that came with it, or if you are afraid its trunk might snap in a heavy wind, then by all means stake it. "Lollipop" trees almost always need staking, and should also be thinned to reduce both the weight and the surface area of their tops. For many trees, a single stake placed in the direction of the prevailing breeze is sufficient, but severely weak-trunked or big-headed trees will need two, placed perpendicular to the wind.

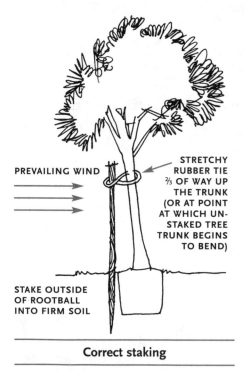

PREVAILING WIND

STRETCHY RUBBER TIE ⅔ OF WAY UP THE TRUNK (OR AT POINT AT WHICH UN-STAKED TREE TRUNK BEGINS TO BEND)

STAKE OUTSIDE OF ROOTBALL INTO FIRM SOIL

Correct staking

Use any stout eight- or ten-foot stakes (I like "lodgepole" stakes). Start them just outside the root ball of the tree, and drive them until they are fully anchored into firm, undisturbed soil. If you have only a few stakes to pound, a sledgehammer is fine. But a post-pounder works much better (and is easier on the arms, wrists, neck, shoulder, and back . . .). If you are fond of your head, you will slide the post-pounder over the end of the stake while said stake

QUICK TIP

Extremely large trees (anything over a fifteen-gallon size—and you shouldn't really attempt anything larger than a thirty-six-inch box) will require special handling. You don't carry trees this size, but rather move them by "walking" them from side to side. The only way to get them out of the container is to cut the steel bands that bind the box. Do this once the tree is perched on the edge of its hole. Note the best face of the tree and calculate its placement so that when the tree is maneuvered into the hole its best side will be facing your primary vantage point. Once the tree is in the hole, it will be very difficult to turn it even a few degrees in any direction.

is lying on the ground. *Then*, with the pounder safely stabilized by the stake, raise both above your head and into pounding position.

Attach the trunk of the tree to the stakes about two-thirds of the way up the trunk, using approved tree ties made from recycled tires or other rubber materials. *Never* use wire, rope, clothesline, or *anything* but rubber; these materials will cut through the bark in short order, causing grievous and irreparable harm.

The purpose of staking a tree is only to support its trunk until it becomes self-supporting. To hasten that day, the trunk must be able to move freely about in order to build up its caliper. So do not make the beginner's (and many a professional's) error of staking the tree so tightly that it is immobilized. The trunk should be able to move several inches in all directions. I have actually seen trees that were staked too tightly that had developed *reverse* taper (the trunk was actually fatter at the top, above the tree tie, where it could flex and move).

Be sure to remove the stakes in a year or two. How many times have I seen trees holding up their stakes, instead of vice versa? Or a tree girdled by its own ties? The damage done from improper staking can be worse than the risk of leaving a tree not staked at all.

Balled and Burlapped Plants

In some parts of the country, balled and burlapped plants are commonplace, but here in California they are the exception to the container plant rule. Both balled and burlapped and bare root plants are "field grown"; that is, they are grown in the ground and then dug up for transport to market. Nearly all our "b and b" stock comes from the great nursery plantations to our north in Oregon and Washington. Large, well-formed specimen trees and nearly full-sized shrubs are shipped down here in the winter dormant season, when they are best able to withstand the shock of excavation. You can get some beautiful, and often rare plants from such stock.

The best thing about field-grown plants is that they rarely have the root problems all too common with container stock—circling roots from overcrowding, for example. The downside is that such plants must be planted with care, since they just *lost* a good portion of those roots. Trees and even shrubs are more likely to need staking, since their roots aren't large or heavy enough to anchor the plant.

Balled and burlapped plants must be placed in their planting hole *still wrapped.* If you attempt to unwrap them, the rootball, such as it is, will almost certainly disintegrate, and you'll lose most of the valuable remaining roots. The preferred technique, then, is to place the intact rootball with its wrapping of burlap in the hole, then cut the twine, at least directly around the crown, and backfill. The twine and burlap will both rot in no time.

Bare-Root Plants

The most important thing to remember with bare-root plants is that those roots must never dry out. Since they have no soil to protect them, they can shrivel in a jiffy. If you can't plant right away, you should "heel them in": Lay them on the ground or in a trench and cover the roots with soil, compost, leaves, newspapers,

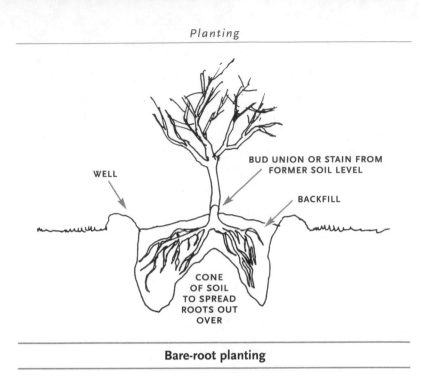

WELL

BUD UNION OR STAIN FROM
FORMER SOIL LEVEL

BACKFILL

CONE
OF SOIL
TO SPREAD
ROOTS OUT
OVER

Bare-root planting

or whatever, then water well and keep the roots moist until planting.

Always soak your bare-root plants in a big bucket of water before planting them. If you've just gotten them from the nursery, a ten- or fifteen-minute soak may be fine, but if they've had an opportunity to dry out, they'll need a couple of hours.

Bare-root plants, by definition, lack a ball of soil around their roots, and so placing them at the correct height can be tricky. Look for stains along the trunk indicating the previous soil depth. If you can't discern such a mark, then use the point at which the roots start to branch from the trunk (the crown) as your reference point, and place the plant so that that spot is a little higher than the surrounding grade.

With bare-root plants, you should make a cone of soil at the bottom of your hole and spread the roots out over it, then backfill and create a well as usual. It doesn't hurt to water once when the hole is half backfilled, and again when it is full, in order to ensure that there are no air pockets next to those vulnerable roots.

TRYING CIRCUMSTANCES

My working horticultural philosophy is best summed up by the dictum "don't fight Mother Nature." And then I'd like to add "because you'll lose!" So if you are trying to create Versailles in the Sierras, or grow roses in the land of Bambi, you might just be better off moving. Landscaping is supposed to be fun, remember? So be nice to yourself and make peace with what you've got. Having said that, here are a few low-stress ways to deal with two of the most aggravating site conditions you'll encounter: steep slopes, and varmints.

Hillsides

Planting on a slope presents special challenges. To begin with, plants in cans have an annoying way of rolling down the hill. So do your supplies, the dirt from the hole, and sometimes even your own embarrassed self.

It can also be very difficult to plant at the correct depth on a slope. Because there never seems to be enough dirt for a good well, if you plant high (as I've previously instructed you to), the plant can dry out. But planting low has its own dangers.

The trick to working on hillsides is to create a little terrace for each plant. Always dig your soil from the uphill side of the planting hole and deposit it on the downhill. In addition, the slope directly above the hole should be graded back to a less steep "angle of repose" so that soil can't erode down onto the plant. This will give you more dirt for the area below the plant, where you really need it to create a mighty earthen berm to keep the water in. Basically, at each hole you cut and fill to create a flat spot in which to plant.

On extremely steep slopes, it's not a bad idea to look into some of the erosion-control materials that are available these days. Probably the most useful is jute netting, which you lay across a slope and staple down, and then plant through it. You still use mulch on top of it, but it helps prevent gullying on

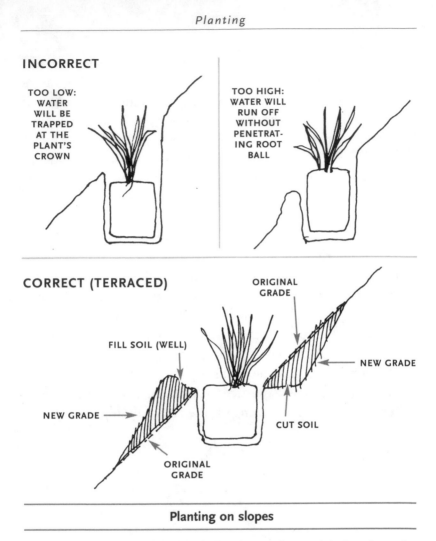

INCORRECT

TOO LOW: WATER WILL BE TRAPPED AT THE PLANT'S CROWN

TOO HIGH: WATER WILL RUN OFF WITHOUT PENETRAT- ING ROOT BALL

CORRECT (TERRACED)

ORIGINAL GRADE

FILL SOIL (WELL)

NEW GRADE

NEW GRADE

CUT SOIL

ORIGINAL GRADE

Planting on slopes

vulnerable hillsides. It also helps keep the mulch in place (by providing friction on the soil surface).

If you are irrigating a slope with drip irrigation, make sure your emitters are on the uphill side of the plant so that the water moves downhill onto the root ball.

Gophers

The only sane way to garden in gopher country is to plant everything in wire. Trapping and poisoning, those ultrasonic vibrating doohickeys, magical anti-gopher plants . . . I'm sorry, you guys, but none of those devices actually work. Sure, you can kill the gopher that just got your prize-winning rose, but I have news for you. His aunts and uncles, nieces and nephews, and even second cousins twice removed have been biding their time for a chance at his estate. Gophers are territorial animals, and as soon as a vacancy occurs, you will have new tenants. So starvation, not execution, is your best tactic. Besides, they are very cute animals. Do you really want their innocent blood on your pacifist hands?

The wire that seems to work best is called "aviary wire." The holes are the right diameter for keeping out our furry friends, and the wire is galvanized, which means it won't rust to dust when it has been buried for a couple of months. Some people swear by hardware cloth, which is even thicker and denser, but I find it too hard to fold, and the dirt doesn't pass through it, which creates air pockets at planting time.

The preferred technique is to simply wrap the entire root ball in wire. To do this, you must cut a rectangular length of wire to the correct dimensions, then roll the root ball up in it and fold

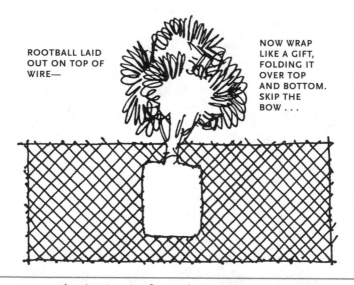

ROOTBALL LAID OUT ON TOP OF WIRE—

NOW WRAP LIKE A GIFT, FOLDING IT OVER TOP AND BOTTOM. SKIP THE BOW . . .

Planting in wire for gophers (before wrapping)

the wire over the top and bottom—somewhat like wrapping a gift. It is important that the top of the plant be covered as well as the bottom. A lot of people buy ready-made gopher baskets and then neglect to fold the top over, and the gophers just jump in and have at it. Speaking of these baskets, they are too expensive to use for an entire landscape, and I find it harder to avoid air pockets when backfilling between them and the root ball than when the root ball is simply wrapped.

WIRE WRAPPED ON TOP, SIDES, AND BOTTOM OF ROOTBALL

After wrapping

The purpose of the wire is really not so much to provide total protection as it is to give the plant a fighting chance while it is establishing a more widespread root system. A four-inch chunk of root is no great loss to a full-grown fruit tree; in the case of a young sapling, on the other hand, that's half its root system. Over time, nearly all a plant's roots will have grown past any wire barrier, which may have even disintegrated, but by then the chance of a gopher destroying most of the roots is greatly reduced. They just can't eat that much in one sitting. Unless it's a rose or a fruit tree. I've seen a ten-foot plum (mine, I'm sorry to say) lying on the ground, its taproot severed just below the crown.

Deer (or Other Hooved Vermin)

The only way to garden in deer country without getting yourself hauled off to the sanatorium is to surround your entire property in eight-foot-high chain-link, patrol it with undernourished Rottweilers, and install automatic sprinklers triggered by motion sensors. Hah hah, just kidding! You can also move.

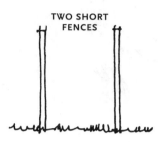

TWO SHORT FENCES

ONE SHORT FENCE WITH BAFFLE

WIRE BAFFLE

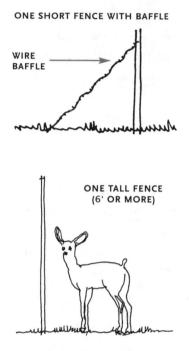

ONE TALL FENCE (6' OR MORE)

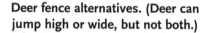

Deer fence alternatives. (Deer can jump high or wide, but not both.)

Okay, so you like your house and want to stay. If you are a serious plant lover, you will get either or both the fence and the dogs (any large dog will do—even a fat old Lab), since the only truly deerproof plants are the ones the deer haven't gotten around to eating yet.

Deer fence should be a minimum of six feet high, more if deer can access it from upslope. If this conjures images of San Quentin and Pelican Bay, then consider using a shorter double fence (deer can jump high or they can jump wide, but not both), or a lower fence with a baffle to extend its width. Your local farm advisor's desk should have plans for such fences.

There is one other technique you can use for trees or tall shrubs that will eventually grow higher than browsing pests or pets (and I do mean pets—horses and llamas can denude foliage much higher than a deer's five-foot reach). The trick is to plant in cages. This is a good way to establish trees in pastures, and to protect young trees—even allegedly deerproof ones—from the damage caused by bucks rubbing their itchy, horny heads on the tender bark.

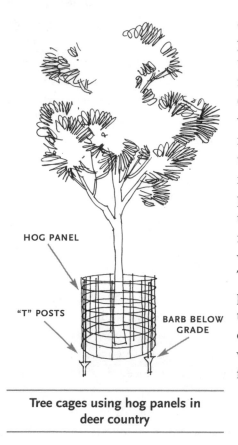

HOG PANEL

"T" POSTS

BARB BELOW GRADE

Tree cages using hog panels in deer country

The easiest and strongest method to protect your plants in this way is to buy twenty- by four-foot or wider "hog panels" (sections of very thick galvanized wire) and a few metal "T posts." You need to go to a place that sells ranching or fencing supplies. Drive a T post into the ground about four feet from the tree or shrub and wire the panel to it tightly. Then slowly bend the panel around to encircle the plant and attach the other end to the stake as well. Use a second stake for additional support at the opposite end of the loop you have created. These panels work much better than simple wire fencing because they are so rigid. Use taller panels for larger (and longer-necked) animals, or use two panels to create a larger circle and more distance from the plant.

MULCH: THE GIFT THAT KEEPS ON GIVING

If there is one rule I have on every single job that we do, it is "No bare dirt." When we are done with a place, you will not see dirt anywhere, from one fence line to the next. The reason for this is that to leave dirt naked is to welcome weeds into your garden. It is so much easier to lay down mulch once every four years or so than to pull weeds three or four times per annum that I really don't understand why more people don't embrace mulching as enthusiastically as they do vitamins, or prayer, or wearing seat belts . . .

What *is* mulch? Mulch is any material applied to the soil surface in order to prevent weeds. So, technically, the black plastic that farmers use around strawberry plants is mulch, although what's more commonly used are organic materials such as bark, compost, or straw. But I've seen people use newspapers, old carpet, and even wool to keep weeds at bay. Mulch materials may vary widely, but all mulches work in the same way. Applied at the proper thickness, they inhibit the germination of weed seeds by blocking light from reaching the soil. They won't work, though, if you don't put enough down. With most materials, the mulch needs to be applied at least two and a half inches thick.

What's great about mulch is that any weeds that do make it through are really easy to pull, because they're mostly rooted in loose mulch, not dense soil. Mulch works best in preventing annual weeds (those that come up every year from seed). If applied thickly enough, though, it can even thwart perennial enemies such as Bermuda grass and blackberries.

Of course, mulch has many other beneficial qualities. It greatly reduces the amount of water your plants will need by insulating their roots and inhibiting evaporation from the soil surface. Organic mulches release nutrients into the soil as they break down (after first pulling nitrogen *from* the soil, however, in some cases). And all mulches lend a finished look to your landscape, covering clods of soil and unifying the garden, much like a single type of carpeting used throughout a house.

When I first started gardening, mulching was a relatively new and radical concept. People still cultivated their soil to eliminate weeds and for the supposed benefit of oxygenating it. Back then, the only material available around here for mulching was oversized hunks of redwood bark. Since then, however, the redwood by-product business has expanded to include chips in particle sizes from practically dust to those same big chunks, as well as "double-ground" bark (rudely referred to as "gorilla hair" by ignorami and cognoscenti alike).

But better yet for us mulch enthusiasts have been the laws requiring communities to reduce their green waste. Now mulch sources include recycled lumber (splintery), turkey and mushroom farms (smelly), tree companies (great), and the dump (variable). My own particular favorite is a locally produced material called "arbor mulch." It is essentially tree-company waste that has been run through the chipper a few times and then partially decomposed. It's cheap, looks completely natural, and has a good assortment of particle sizes. (Smaller particles block more light from reaching the soil but tend to move around; larger particles, especially fibrous ones, knit together and help keep the mulch in place.)

Mulches vary greatly in price and appearance. Let both those factors help you decide which type to use, but also keep in mind a few others. Small round particles move. Pea gravel, for example, is easily scattered off a pathway. For this reason, crushed-rock products work better for paths than do river-rounded rocks; their sharp edges cause the rock to pack down and stay put. Similarly, small bark pieces, particularly those of a uniform size, are more likely to get kicked out of place than long, stringy, or irregular particles. Bark also "floats." So limit your use of such premium mulches to small, highly visible areas where their beauty will compensate for their drawbacks.

Using compost as mulch is great for the soil, but any mulch that breaks down that quickly needs to be replaced frequently. Rock mulches are the best choice if you never want to mulch again (but they are hard to keep clean). If you are mulching on a slope, choose a fibrous mulch such as the much-maligned gorilla hair. It mats down into a feltlike substance and stays put better than any other material I know.

Never, ever use weed fabric under mulch. It seems like such a good idea, doesn't it? And every hardware-store guy in the country promotes it. Well, they're wrong. It does work well, for a while. But then it gets loose, flaps around, and looks like litter. Later, when you decide to redo your landscape (and believe me, it'll look so bad you'll want to), you'll find the stuff is almost impossible to remove. It stops shovels cold, gets wrapped up in the tines of the tiller, and, buried under dirt, defies any attempt to dislodge it. Can you tell I hate the stuff?

The problem is that most people simply don't use enough mulch, so they get weeds and think fabric must be the answer. Use three or four inches of mulch (up to six inches under mature oaks) and you'll be just fine. The only time I use weed fabric is under a very heavy rock mulch, such as cobbles—and even then I staple it down well, especially at the edges.

Make sure to grade well, for the last time (hurrah!), before applying mulch. Every high spot will become a place where the mulch is too thin, every low spot a place where mulch has been wasted. Part of this final grading, too, should be to ensure you have a mulch layer's worth of height difference between your final soil level and any paved areas,

QUICK MULCHING TIP

Aim for a uniform thickness throughout. Don't rake a given pile in such a way as to cover all the nearby bare ground if there isn't enough mulch to cover it to the correct thickness. If you end up with a too-thin layer of mulch in an area, you'll never know where to find it later, when you realize you ordered way too much and may have to start giving it away to the neighbors. No, what you want to do is spread the mulch according to the correct thickness. Leave places bare if there isn't enough so that you can easily find and fill them in later.

ESSENTIAL MULCHING TIP

Remember how I harped on planting heights and crown rot? Make sure you don't cover up the crown of any plant, particularly trees, with mulch. This is especially relevant for the finer-textured types of mulch, which really hold in the moisture. What we do is leave the entire root-ball surface of the plant exposed and mulch-free. With established trees, we keep clear an area at least eight inches in every direction from the trunk.

so that when the mulch is in place it will be at or slightly below the level of your patio, sidewalk, or whatever. That way it'll stay put and you won't have to resort to the frequently witnessed expedient of installing cheesy little bender-board borders to keep the bark off your exposed aggregate.

When you are ready for delivery of your mulch, remember some of the hints for the application of bulk materials I discussed in the section of Chapter 5 titled "Amendments." Most important is the formula I gave there for calculating the amount to order, so I'll repeat it: Multiply your total square footage by the number of inches thick you'd like and divide that sum by 324 to get the number of cubic yards needed.

Planting and mulching are easy, really. It's all the steps that precede them which are difficult, and which determine their success or failure. I encouraged you to do a proper plan for your landscape because if you put a shade-loving plant in full sun it will scorch, and if you put a drought-tolerant plant next to a lawn it will yellow. I stressed the importance of grading before planting because if plants are in a low spot, they may rot. I preached so long about irrigation because if your irrigation system is less than perfect, your plants will alternately drown or wither. I spent a whole chapter on soil preparation because if your soil is garbage, your plants will fail to thrive.

A fine garden, like the ecosystem it mimics, is made up of many interdependent components. A garden is also like a chain—only as strong as its weakest link. So, if you've neglected to read the other chapters of this book before planting, it's not too late! Your plants will thank you.

Chapter 8

Lawns

Your Own Magic Carpet

These are difficult times for those who love lawns. If you have childhood memories of summer thunderstorms, your vision of domestic bliss is almost certain to include generous swards of velvety green turf. Even native Westerners can fall prey to the charms of soft, moist grass underfoot. Lawn, turf, grass, or sod: By any name, these plants drink a lot of water. Add gasoline to mow, fertilizer to green, and pesticides to perfect them, and maybe you should get an environmental impact report before you even break ground. What's a conscientious person to do?

One thing to do is to limit your use of lawn to its best applications. There certainly is no better surface for indolent infants and toddling toddlers, for athletic eight-year-olds and barefoot teenage bathing beauties. The one quality grass has that other green groundcovers lack is its walkability. So design your lawn areas for active uses rather than simply as a green backdrop. If your lawn is just for show, replace it with plantings.

Another way to mitigate the environmental impact of using grass is to relinquish the quest for the perfect lawn. In fact, the symptoms of neglect that cause so many people to despair—weediness, brown or yellow spots, and so on—are usually easily eliminated by following proper cultural practices rather than resorting to insecti-, fungi- and herbi-cides. Give your lawn what it wants—adequate water, and regular mowing and fertilization—and it will be thick and healthy enough to repel hungry pests, debilitating diseases, and invading weeds.

LAWN TRUTHS

- *Lawn Truth Number One.* You only get one chance to properly prepare your soil. If you lay sod over lousy dirt, you can't go back later and work in amendments, and you'll have to water and fertilize constantly to keep the grass alive.
- *Lawn Truth Number Two.* A lawn is like a blank canvas for your every irrigation mistake. Because turf is composed of millions of tiny individual grass plants, if any one of those plants is missed by a sprinkler, even by as little as an inch, it will die. (Put a much larger plant in the same spot and chances are it will get enough water overall to survive.) When designing irrigation for your lawns, make sure that every area gets watered by at least two different heads, and don't take chances with the number of heads you use on a line. Make sure you have that head-to-head coverage I discussed in Chapter 6.
- *Lawn Truth Number Three.* Your lawn can never be too level. Mowed turf will reveal every dip and hump of your final grade, so be certain that your irrigation trenches are properly backfilled (soak them with water when half filled and then again when full) and that any filled areas have been compacted or allowed to settle.

GRADING, DRAINAGE, AND SOIL PREP FOR TURF

The steps for installing grass will follow the same sequence as those for the rest of the landscape, with a few special caveats for each procedure. As in the overall landscape, grading is the first step: You should rough-grade your lawn area for proper drainage before preparing the soil or installing irrigation, then again after each of those operations. It is okay to run your swales through grass, but be aware that mowing during the rainy season or after irrigation may be difficult if there is not good flow down the length of the channel. The weight of a mower can really tear up soggy areas. Make sure that you allow at least a 3 percent slope (see Chapter 4) across any turf surface to allow good runoff. If you need subterranean drainage, the lawn is a good place to put your drainage grates, since the grass acts as a natural filter, preventing debris from obstructing the flow of water.

Irrigation for lawn areas follows the same principles outlined in Chapter 6. Don't cut corners here, since trying to retrofit an inadequate system after your grass is in will mean destroying the turf. Use pop-up heads in lawn areas, since above-ground heads on fixed risers are both hazardous and likely to get broken. Be sure to use swing joints at each sprinkler head, particularly where you anticipate lots of traffic (either human or—heaven forbid!—vehicular). Just don't bother setting the height of each head until after your *final* grading pass, right before you're ready to sod or seed. Once that time has come, set the heads about one-half to three-quarters of an inch above the surrounding grade so that they will be at the same height as the grass once it's established.

Soil preparation for turf needs to be meticulous. Any irregularities in your soil prep will show up on the finished lawn. If one part of your grass is growing in rich, fertile topsoil and another is underlain by flinty subsoil, the former area will be thick and green and the latter thin and yellow. When conditioning soil for a lawn, aim for uniformity above all.

Since you will expend a great deal of effort ensuring that your final grade is flat and level, the use of screened and amended topsoil is worth considering. It is just so much easier to rake smooth than clod-prone native soils. Plus you can then skip all the work of tilling, bringing in compost, and then tilling again; it's all been done for you at the topsoil factory. Just be sure when using topsoil that you use enough—at least three inches thick throughout the entire lawn area.

Border Patrol

It is usually easier to install your edging after all tilling is completed, and before the topsoil is brought in, if it is to be used. Bender board makes a fine but short-lived (five years or so) border when installed mostly below grade, three or more pieces thick. Plastic imitators last forever but are harder to install correctly. They shrink and swell with temperature changes, and they lack the rigidity needed to create beautiful curves, and so must be installed with due diligence. I've had better luck with the thicker (two-by-four) size.

By far the best-looking (but most expensive) edgings are brick and concrete. If you choose bricks, though, do it right and mortar them to a concrete base, rather than just laying them in the dirt—they'll look better and last longer. And avoid the

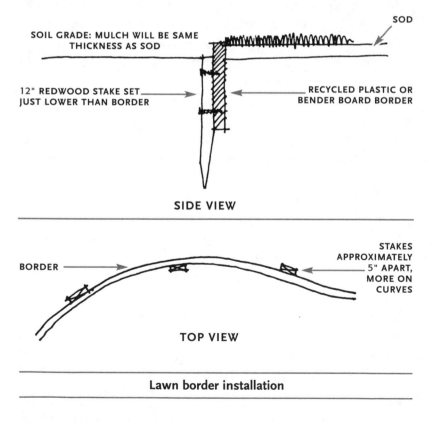

Lawn border installation

temptation to pour a concrete border (or base) at the same time as your other concrete work unless you can be certain the grade for the edging won't need to change—for example, if topsoil is to be brought in.

Avoid using rocks to edge your lawn. You need a smooth, continuous division between the turf and any other materials. Grass will grow in between rocks, where it is hard to trim even with hand trimmers, much less a weed-eater. You can also opt for a borderless lawn, but be aware that many lawn grasses can invade flowerbeds, becoming pernicious weeds.

Setting the Stage

Once your soil is ready and your edging in, you must do your final grade, level, and roll before laying sod or broadcasting seed. First, grade one more time to ensure positive drainage. Create a half-inch to a one-inch drop below any borders or edges so that when the sod is laid it will be flush with them. For a seed lawn, make the soil level with your edging. (See illustration, next page.) Then level your soil surface to eliminate high and low spots, so that it is flat. This is the one time in the landscaping process when you are allowed to rake up and dump clods (though if there are more clods than dirt, don't even bother, since most will disappear when rolled, in the next step). And yes, you should aim for perfection.

QUICK TIP

It may be worth investing in an extra-large rake if yours is a very large lawn. Such an implement (often simply called a "land-scaper's rake") is wide enough to shave high spots and fill low ones as you drag it along the soil surface. Where can you get one? At your local friendly landscape/ irriga-tion supply place, of course.

You'll really be able to see (and feel, under foot) every over-looked hump and dip.

Rent a lawn roller (some places will loan one out for free if you buy your sod from them) and fill it about two-thirds full of water. Roll your future lawn area slowly, in two directions (the

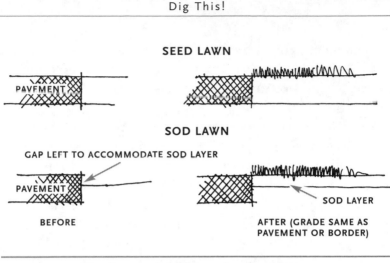

Grading at edges for seed and sod lawns

second perpendicular to the first). Some areas will compact more than others, so afterwards you should re-level and then roll again. Repeat as necessary. And no waffling: You want your finished grade to be as flat as that other breakfast food, the pancake.

Before planting your grass, either sod or seed, you should fertilize. This is a great time to practice the broadcasting skills you'll need for the life of your lawn, because you'll actually be able to see where the stuff falls as you spread it.

If you buy your lawn food at a commercial landscape supply house (perhaps where you purchased your irrigation supplies), you can be assured of getting fertilizer that works well (after all, the pros are using the stuff) at about half the hardware store cost. Also, pick up a hand-held "whirlybird" type spreader. Do *not* use a drop-style spreader,

> **QUICK WHIRLYBIRD TIP**
> Begin cranking before you open the chute that lets the granules out, or you'll have a spill. And the minute you open that chute, begin walking. Walk at an even pace, and close the chute at the end of each pass. Don't despair if you still have material left over—that's much better than coming up short (which means you overapplied it somewhere). Just continue broadcasting at yet another angle, trying to cover the entire lawn with each new direction so that you have uniform coverage.

unless you like striped lawns (yellow where the fertilizer missed, green where it's about right, and dead brown where you double-dosed). Drop spreaders—the staple of garage sales everywhere—are right up there with weed fabric on my list of hardware store peeves. You won't even see them for sale where the pros shop—and what does *that* tell you?

Calculate how much fertilizer to apply based on the square footage of your lawn area. The best way to ensure even distribution is to use about half of that amount of fertilizer walking back and forth in one direction (say, north and south) and then the rest in a direction at right angles to the first (east and west). The goal is to broadcast a small amount at a time so that you don't use it all up on only one portion of the lawn. In fact, until you get the hang of it, use the lowest setting (the one that releases the least amount of fertilizer)—that way you can be *sure* not to overapply your material.

SEED OR SOD?

Hardly anyone except the neurotically thrifty ever puts in a seed lawn anymore. But it's a shame, really, because to grow a lawn from seed is to witness one of the true miracles of horticulture. It is so gratifying to observe the daily transformation of a muddy plain into a grassy green jewel. Plus, the resulting lawn is, if anything, healthier and more vigorous than one started from sod transplants, since it grows up on, and is adapted to, your own soil.

I think the reason so many people are afraid of seed lawns (we'll assume a lack of patience is not the only issue) is that they don't fully understand the process by which those delicate little sprouts become tough, hardy turf. They get discouraged when the seed germinates unevenly and looks like a balding pate with psoriasis. Every weed seems to portend failure.

Seed lawns require faith. Yes, not all the seeds will sprout in unison. But wait another week and today's bare spot will probably show a hopeful fuzz of green. And yes, that's a weed. But most weeds can't tolerate being mowed, or don't like being crowded by the grass, and will disappear over time. You really do need faith. *And* patience.

Sod lawns, on the other hand, are a miracle of sorts, too. There is simply no greater transformation than that which occurs in one day's hard work laying sod. In the space of a few hours, a barren dust bowl can be transformed into an inviting green oasis. If you have kids and dogs eager to play, or a garden party coming up in a few weeks, you really can't afford to wait around for a seed lawn to become viable. So weigh your alternatives and decide what works best for your budget, circumstances, and temperament. (If by any chance it's winter when you need to put your lawn in, your choice just got easier—you'll have to use sod.)

Sodding: Instant Gratification

If you decide to lay sod, you will need to order it a few days before you want delivery. Figure out how much you need by measuring your area very carefully, and then adding a few more rolls to allow for mistakes, waste from cutting, and so on. I'd always rather have a little extra to give to the neighbors than come up short and have to scrounge around the scrap pile. For a thousand-square-foot lawn, I'd get four or five extra rolls (most rolls are ten square feet).

Once your sod is delivered, work fast, enlisting the help of all nearby able bodies. See the tag on the pallet that says "Sod is perishable"? They're not lying! Sod left rolled up on a hot day will compost itself in no time. Keep unused rolls moist, and don't stop slapping the stuff down till it's all done.

Start at the farthest straight edge. Farthest, so you don't have to walk across your newly laid sod afterward. Straight edge because the worst thing you can do when laying sod is to have to do a lot of cutting. Sod cutting produces more blisters, faster, than just about any other chore I can imagine.

If your lawn is so curvaceous that there *are* no straight edges,

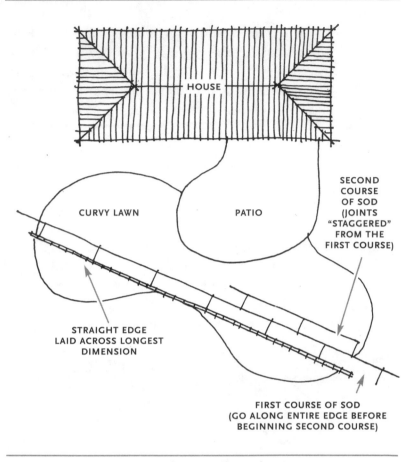

HOUSE

SECOND COURSE OF SOD (JOINTS "STAGGERED" FROM THE FIRST COURSE)

CURVY LAWN

PATIO

STRAIGHT EDGE LAID ACROSS LONGEST DIMENSION

FIRST COURSE OF SOD (GO ALONG ENTIRE EDGE BEFORE BEGINNING SECOND COURSE)

Laying sod on curvilinear lawns

---

make one. Lay a two-by-four or stretch a string across somewhere and start laying the strips lengthwise along it from that point. For the same reason, do not start laying sod at two different ends of the yard and hope to meet in the middle. We did that. Once.

A couple more tips: Stagger the edges (as in laying bricks) so you don't have a continuous seam running the whole length of the lawn. Aim to have neither gaps (which dry out) nor overlaps (which spoil the grade) between strips. (And last but not least, yes, the green side faces *up*.)

Once the bulk of the lawn is laid, you should cut all the edges to fit tight against your borders. If you reined in your creative impulses as advised, you should be trimming *only* edges. Find yourself needing to cut every single strip down the middle of the lawn, where there is no nice border to guide you? A sharp knife will be your new best friend. Keep a sharpener handy nearby—you'll be using it more than you ever imagined.

When all the sod is down and the edges are cut, roll the lawn again. Fill the roller only half full this time, and roll only once. The purpose of rolling is to press the roots of the grass into good contact with the soil.

Clean up all your scraps and then water. I don't mean turn on the sprinklers for a few minutes, I mean *water*. Soak. Drench. Inundate. You should water so thoroughly and deeply and long that the soil beneath the sod becomes saturated. I often water by hand rather than relying on the irrigation so that I can make sure any particularly dry spots get water immediately. In fact, if it is a hot day and you were unable to draft a sufficient number

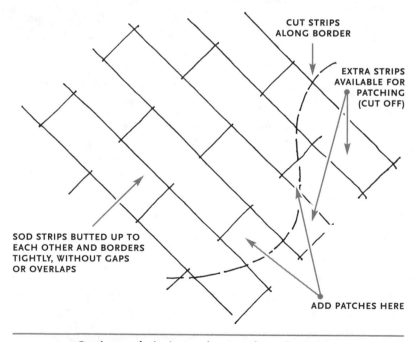

Cutting and piecing sod strips along the border

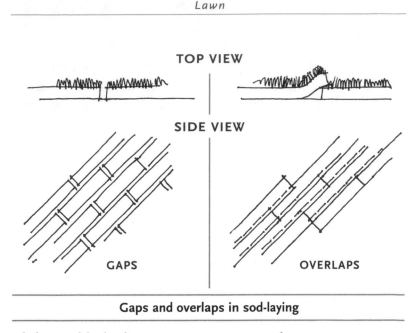

TOP VIEW

SIDE VIEW

GAPS

OVERLAPS

Gaps and overlaps in sod-laying

of those able bodies, you may want to do some emergency watering before you are completely done laying every strip. Look out for areas where the grass appears dark and dull. That's what turf looks like when it wilts.

Adjust your heads and nozzles to make sure they cover the lawn as planned. I always allow for a little overspray onto nearby walks and plants, so that if there is a breeze, the lawn edges are still watered. This is the time too to program your timer.

Keep your new lawn wet for the first crucial couple of weeks. In spring through fall, this may mean twice daily irrigation. Because the soil will be mushy mud under the sod strips, keep people and heavy pets off newly installed turf, or all your careful grading will be ruined. Once your sod is rooted (it is amazing how quickly this happens—lift up a strip to see), you can start tapering off on the watering (in about ten days). But don't even think of mowing until your lawn is dry enough to walk on without sinking in and leaving marks.

Seeding: A Holistic Approach

The best times of year to sow a lawn from seed are spring and fall, when the temperatures are mild. But summer will work if you are willing to water three times a day if there's a heat wave. Just don't try to seed in the winter. The seed won't sprout when the temperatures are low, so you'll have months of eroding mud to contend with. In Northern California, I wouldn't sow a lawn after October or before April, as a rule.

The process of planting grass from seed parallels that for sod right up until the point at which the choice must be made. So prepare the soil, install your edgings and irrigation, and grade, level, roll, and fertilize as instructed above.

For a seed lawn, you will be much happier if you use topsoil, since your native soil is most likely infested with weed seeds just waiting to sprout. If you *must* use your own soil, pre-soak it to germinate those weed seeds, and once they've sprouted, kill them. Spraying with an appropriate herbicide (follow the directions) is the easiest, because you can do all your soil preparation, turn on the sprinklers, and spray the resulting green weed fuzz in a couple of weeks. The next day, without further ado, you can seed and top-dress. If you'd prefer to avoid herbicides, however, you should soak and sprout the weeds before your final grading, and then lightly hoe them up, grade, level, and roll. Be careful not to hoe too deeply; and certainly don't till the weeds under, or you'll expose a whole *new* crop of weed seeds to contend with.

Decide what type of grass to plant. In general, fescues are a good bet for full sun and bluegrass for part shade, but don't let me keep you from exploring all your options. Just be sure that the grass you select is adapted to your zone (call your local Master Gardeners).

You will also need a fine-textured compost to cover the seed after it's been spread, protecting it from birds and erosion and helping to warm the soil. Most bagged products are sufficiently uniform and fine-textured for this purpose. Figure on a thickness throughout of an eighth to a quarter of an inch.

Using the same whirlybird spreader you used to fertilize, broadcast the grass seed as evenly as you can, throwing out a small amount at a time in two or more different directions (as you did when fertilizing) until it is distributed uniformly. Avoid doing this on a breezy day—the seed will blow off target and you'll have grass growing in all sorts of places you'd rather it didn't.

Now, top-dress over it with your compost. Special spreaders do exist for this, but they are hard to find. So you will probably need to spread the compost by hand, which is a pain. For small areas, fill up a five-gallon plastic bucket and broadcast carefully by hand. For larger areas, you will want to spread the compost from a wheelbarrow, with a shovel (tread lightly to avoid spoiling your handiwork). Fling each shovelful far and wide, with as much rhythm and grace as you can muster. You must flip your wrist just *so*, causing the material fall evenly in a long, wide arc. This technique takes some practice to perfect, but keep at it.

Take care not too apply the dressing too thickly. Wherever the compost is a little too thick, the seed will take longer to germinate. And if it is *way* too thick, the seed may rot and fail to sprout entirely. Too thin, and the birds will eat the seeds.

Once your lawn is seeded and top-dressed, turn on your irrigation system. Water lightly and frequently at first, ensuring that the soil surface neither dries out nor erodes until the lawn is up and established (at least a couple of weeks). Then reduce the frequency of application while increasing the duration until the soil is dry and firm enough in between watering cycles to bear the weight of a mower.

GREENER GRASS ON *YOUR* SIDE: WATERING, MOWING, AND FEEDING

Although the scope of this book does not include maintenance, a few tips on lawn care will prevent some serious heartache and get you started down the right path. First, a couple of tips on watering. What I've noticed is that people who water by hand water too little, and those with automatic sprinkler systems water too much. Both sod and seed lawns need a tremendous amount of water to get them established, but after that soakings once or twice a week are far better than daily sprinkles. The moisture should penetrate down several inches, encouraging deep root growth (and thus resistance to drought, should one occur either naturally or from timer failure).

Regular mowing is essential to a healthy lawn. A sod lawn should be mowed for the first time as soon as you can do so without leaving ruts. The grass is usually really long by this time, so remove only a third of the height (actually, this is a basic rule for all subsequent mowings too), and then mow again at a lower setting in a few days. Radical haircuts can cause the lawn to go into shock. I always took this on faith until a client of mine reduced her shaggy turf to a crew cut one day, and after that her grass was always thin, yellow, and patchy. And there was nothing to be done but to sod it over again.

Mow your new seed lawn for the first time when the soil is firm and the tips of the grass blades begin to curl. Make sure your mower blades are sharp; a dull blade can tear the young grass plants right out of the dirt. Again, you don't want to remove more than a third of the length, so mow high. You can mow again in a few days. Each time you mow, you cause the grass to "tiller" (thicken up), so your purpose is more than merely cosmetic. Also, each time you mow, you discourage weeds. And there is nothing more satisfying than discouraging a weed.

Finally, feed your lawn. It's just amazing what a dose of fertilizer will do for tired turf. If your grass is bright green where the dog did its business, God is telling you it's time to get out the whirlybird. Your whole *lawn* should be that color.

If you really hate to fertilize, use slow-release stuff (it's expensive, but it will last a whole season). Or, if you use a mulching mower, you may be able to get by with only annual feedings. Otherwise, you should be feeding monthly or so from about

May through September. Or, if you are a less than perfect gardener, you'll fertilize like I do—when the lawn turns yellow. (Hey, between my gopher pals and the Bermuda grass, my quest for turfly perfection ended long ago.)

RENOVATION

Most of the calls I get to replace a lawn are false alarms. I hate talking myself out of work, but often the nastiest-looking turf can be made respectable if not gorgeous by correcting irrigation problems and applying fertilizer. My theory is that if at one time the irrigation worked, it can be made to work again. And feeding can cheer up even the most flea-bitten patch of turf. In fact, many weeds, especially leguminous ones like clover, will disappear over time with judicious fertilization.

I'm not a big believer in the more expensive remedies you'll hear about—thatching and aeration. All too often, hapless homeowners are talked into having their grass worked over by smooth-talking salesmen. The horticultural expertise of these guys is limited, to say the least. What they know best is how to operate the (expensive) equipment they've invested in, and how to convince you that you need them to do it. (They know that we Americans love the quick fix, especially if it involves machinery or technology.) There *are* times when your lawn woes are caused by simple compaction or thatch buildup, but these guys aren't the ones to consult.

The time to redo your grass is when you have more weeds than lawn grass, or if you have truly uncorrectable soil or sprinkler problems. How do you know whether your problems are in this category? Basically, most soil problems (heavy clay, lack of organic matter) cannot be remedied, since how do you work the soil without killing the lawn? And an irrigation system that was poorly designed (too many heads on a line, or heads not well spaced) should be abandoned, since in most cases retrofitting an inadequate existing system takes far more time than installing a functional new one.

The good news about lawn renovation is that you don't necessarily have to remove the old lawn, or even rototill. Why should you? After all, grass and weeds are just organic matter, which we like, remember? The idea is to disturb the ground as little as possible. If you tilled, for example, you'd have to contend with old chunks of dead lawn, which would make raking it smooth difficult.

What you *do* need to do, however, is to kill your tired, weedy old lawn. You can spray it with a nonselective herbicide, or if you'd rather, you can cover the grass with plastic for a few days instead. (This latter technique will kill the lawn and most annual weeds, but perennial weeds such as dandelions, oxalis, and Bermuda grass would need a much longer period of time and significantly hotter temperatures than we usually see in regions such as Northern California.)

Once your old lawn has been snuffed, mow it as low as you can. If you have a weed-eater, trim the old turf down to the dirt. This will make it easier to work the soil in the few areas where this will be necessary (the edges).

The next step is to excavate the dirt back a couple of feet

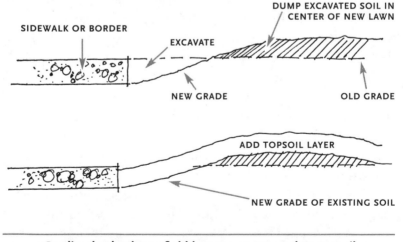

Grading back edges of old lawn to accommodate topsoil

from all existing edges to accommodate the new soil we'll bring in. This assures the application of a uniform thickness of topsoil throughout. The excavated soil can be scattered about in the center of the lawn. Break up or rake out major clods, then cover your old turf with two and a half to three inches of topsoil. The new lawn will be a little higher and slightly convex as a result of these efforts, so obviously you can only renovate your grass in this fashion so many times . . .

If your old irrigation worked, all you'll need to do now is raise the heads. If you need new irrigation, install it before adding the topsoil. If this is the case, there is no need to remove your old system; just unscrew the heads and risers, to avoid confusing them with the new ones.

The one time I do remove old lawns is when they are infested with a particularly unpleasant perennial weed such as Bermuda grass. But you must be meticulous in your pursuit of every bit of the enemy, since with perennial weeds even the weensiest scrap can regenerate into another plant. Sometimes it just isn't worth it. Mound the topsoil especially high and figure you'll replace the lawn again in several years, when the Bermuda reappears, if it still bothers you so much. Me? I have Bermuda in my lawn, or rather, I should say my lawn *is* Bermuda (partly), and I just live with it. Sure it turns brown in the winter, but who's looking? Not me. I'm curled up inside by the fire, reading trashy novels, as I ought to be.

Once you've got functioning irrigation and new soil (and borders if you need them), you can grade, level, roll, and then seed or sod as described earlier in this chapter.

GOPHERS AND MOLES

If you live in rodent country and you're sure you'll never want your lawn area to be anything other than lawn, you can lay down wire before you sod. Just make sure you won't ever need to tear it out, because you won't be able to trench or dig where wire was used, and removing it will be one of the most trying jobs you will ever attempt. Once you have wire enmeshed in grass and dirt, it is too heavy to remove by hand, and the wire tends to rip apart (yet not disappear) if you try to use machinery.

Having now scared you away from using wire, let me say it can be almost as frustrating to contend with the depredations of your local pouch-faced or starry-nosed fauna. So if you decide to thwart the little darlings, here are a few tips.

The longest-lasting material to use is hardware cloth, but it is so heavy that I find it unsatisfactory except in very small areas (it is too hard to eliminate air pockets between the soil and the wire). Galvanized aviary wire is better. Purchase it in six-foot lengths and staple it to the soil using U-shaped jute staples. Make sure to overlap the widths of wire. Unbelievably, gophers will find a half-inch gap if you leave one, even if it's the only opening in three thousand square feet of grass. I sometimes feel sorry for the critters, endlessly tunneling in search of that one breathing hole. But who knows what they do for fun?

I wouldn't recommend using wire with a seed lawn, because once you laid it down you'd need to cover it with soil, which would be hard to do uniformly. And I wouldn't even consider not covering it. The first kid to slide into home plate would get a terrible rash for his heroism, and his parents might be less than totally understanding when it came time to explain.

There is nothing as restful to the eye and refreshing to the nose as a thick, green, healthy new lawn. Well fertilized, it is as verdant as a Swiss meadow in the spring. Freshly watered, it is divinely soft and springy underfoot. Newly mowed, it smells like summer itself. Stroll on it barefoot, and you're a child again. What's not to like?

Sources

American Society of Landscape Architects
636 Eye St. NW, Washington, DC 20001-3736
www.asla.org
202-898-2444

The Bay Area Gardener (website only)
www.gardens.com

California Landscape Contractor's Association (CLCA)
1491 River Park Dr., Suite 100, Sacramento, CA 95815
www.clca.org
916-830-2780

Contractors State Licensing Board
P.O. Box 26000, Sacramento, CA 95826
www.cslb.ca.gov/
800-321-2752

Harmony Farm Supply and Nursery
(irrigation and organic gardening tools, supplies and books; catalog and warehouse)
3244 Highway 116 North, Sebastopol, CA 95472
Mailing address: P.O. Box 9544, Graton, CA 95444
www.harmonyfarm.com
707-823-9125

International Society of Arboriculture, Western Chapter
235 Hollow Oak Dr., Cohasset, CA 95973
www.wc-isa.net
530-892-1118

Irrigation Association
6540 Arlington Blvd., Falls Church, VA 22042-6638
www.irrigation.org
703-536-7080

Master Gardeners (University of California Cooperative Extension; information and
resources, publications for home gardeners)
www.mastergardeners.org

Northern California Master Gardener listings by county:
Alameda County
1131 Harbor Bay Parkway, Alameda 94502
510-567-6812
Contra Costa County
1700 Oak Park Blvd., Bldg. A-2, Pleasant Hill 94523
925-646-6540
Marin County
1682 Novato Blvd., Suite 150-B, Novato 94947
415-499-4204
Monterey County
118 Wilgart Way, Salinas 93901
831-758-4637

San Francisco County
  300 Piedmont Ave., Room 305 A, San Bruno 94066
San Mateo County
  625 Miramontes St., Suite 200, Half Moon Bay 94019
  650-726-9059
Santa Clara County
  1005 Timothy Drive, San Jose 95133
  408-299-2635
Santa Cruz County
  1432 Freedom Blvd., Watsonville 95076
  831-761-4056
Sonoma County
  2604 Ventura Ave., Room 100-P, Santa Rosa 95403
  707-527-2621
Underground Service Alert 800-642-2444

Suggested Readings

Books

Brenzel, Kathleen Norris, ed. *Sunset Western Garden Book*, Seventh edition. Menlo Park, California: Sunset Publishing Corp., 2001.

Coate, Barrie, et al. West. *Water-Conserving Plants & Landscapes for the Bay Area*, second ed. Oakland, California: East Bay Municipal Utility District, 1990.

Smith, Ken. *Western Home Landscaping*, revised ed. Tucson, Arizona: HP Books, 1987.

Stevens, David. *The Garden Design Sourcebook*. London,: Conran Octopus Ltd., 1995.

von Trapp, Sara Jane. *Landscaping from the Ground Up*. Newton, Connecticut: Taunton Press, 1997.

Periodicals

Horticulture magazine

Fine Gardening magazine

Sunset magazine

Index

Pages with illustrations are indicated by **boldface** page numbers.

A

amendments, soil, 123–28
American Society of Landscape
    Architects, 7
angle of repose, 105, 188
anti-siphon valves, 157, 159
arborists, hiring, 12
arbor mulch, 195
arbors, 94–95
Asian-style gardens, 33, 34
assets, examples of, 35
aviary wire, 190
    as lawn protection, 216
availability and price of materials, 59

B

backfilling, 165
    around plants, 178–79
    checklist prior to, 164–65
backflow devices, 157, 158
    protecting from freezing, 158
    size, 158–59
    testing, 161
back trouble, avoiding, 20
back yards, 25–27
balance, 57
balled and burlapped plants, 186
barbecue placement, 50
bare-root plants, 186–87
bark mulch, 194, 195
baseline measuring, **42**, 45
base plans, **39**
    adding secondary features to, 45–47
    alternative, 40
    bubble diagrams, 47–49, **55**
    deciding placement of
        elements in, 49–52
    double-checking, 44–45
    drawing, 37–47
    elements not to show, 37–38
    elements to show, 38–41
    finalizing, 42–47
    measuring items on, 41–42
    scale used for, 41, 44
    sitting area in, 47–49

benches, 94–95
bender board, 202
berms, **26**, 107, **133**–34
    planting wells, 179
"bones" of garden, 31–32, 66
borders. *See* edgings
boulders
    in dry creek beds, **89**
    hiding pond liners with, **79–80**
    installing, 93–94
    placement, **93–94**
brick edgings, 202
bubble diagrams, 47–49, **55**

C

calculations
    amount of fertilizer for lawn, 205
    amount of mulch, 197
    cubic yard, 124
    elevation, 46–47, **46**
    number of drip lines, 144, 45
    number of lines for overhead
        system, 150
    tread/riser ratio, 46, 83–84
    See also measuring
catch basins, 101
chase, **85, 86**
children
    allowing space for, 27
    play equipment for, 51–52
clay soil, 120, 122, 130, 180
clematis, 181
clods, 16–17, 203
collection/dispersion points, 106, 108–9
color contrast, 58–59
compaction, 123
compost
    commercial, 126
    as mulch, 195
    mushroom, 126
    for new lawns, 210, 211
concrete
    edgings, 202
    paving, 85–86
    ponds, 79

Arnold Anchordoguy

ABOUT THE AUTHOR

KATE ANCHORDOGUY is a landscape contractor and designer with more than twenty-five years of experience. She has owned and operated two landscaping companies in Northern California, and has published several articles on gardening and landscaping.

MR

H/03

Dig This!